seared

to perfection

seared

to perfection

the simple art of sealing in flavor

lucy vaserfirer

THE HARVARD COMMON PRESS

Boston, Massachusetts

THE HARVARD COMMON PRESS
535 Albany Street
Boston, Massachusetts 02118
www.harvardcommonpress.com

Printed in the United States of America
Printed on acid-free paper

Library of Congress Cataloging-in-Publication Data
Vaserfirer, Lucy.
Seared to perfection : the simple art of sealing in flavor / Lucy Vaserfirer.
p. cm.
Includes index.
ISBN 978-1-55832-398-8 (alk. paper)
1. Sautéing. 2. Cookery (Meat) I. Title.
TX689.4.V37   2009
641.7'7—dc22
2009050011

Special bulk-order discounts are available on this and other Harvard Common Press books.
Companies and organizations may purchase books for premiums or resale, or may arrange a
custom edition, by contacting the Marketing Director at the address above.

Jacket photographs—*front:* Rib-eye Steaks with Caramelized Onions, page 20;
spine: Pork Chops with Brandy-Mustard Cream Sauce, page 43; *back:* Pineapple with Vanilla Ice Cream
and Coconut-Caramel Sauce, page 128 ; Halibut with Roasted Red Pepper Coulis, page 93

Jacket photographs by Joyce Oudkerk Pool
Food and prop styling by Heidi Gitner
Book design by Ralph Fowler Design

2   4   6   8   10   9   7   5   3   1

contents

acknowledgments

I extend a warm thank-you to Janie Hibler for her support and advice. Janie's kind words of encouragement convinced me to stop dreaming about this book and actually write it.

Thanks to Kathy Block-Brown, Bekki Callaway, Erin Keplinger, Sarah Keplinger, Cosh Ng, and Ian and Heather Penny for testing recipes and giving lots of thoughtful feedback.

Thank you to my brother, Andrew, for testing recipes and proofreading the text, and for being my biggest fan.

I'm so lucky to have my husband, Barry, who through it all believes in me. He's always the first person to lay eyes on any of my writing and to taste all of my recipe tests, and he gives me his honest opinion (even if it's slightly biased). He also functions as my kitchen assistant; all of the cooking times in the book are accurate thanks to his careful timekeeping.

I am ever grateful to my agent, Clare Pelino, for her patience, guidance, and support through this very long process.

And a big thank-you to my editor, Harriet Bell, from whom I learned so much. I am a stronger and more confident writer thanks to her.

Finally, my sincere thanks to Bruce Shaw, Jane Dornbusch, Valerie Cimino, and everyone else at The Harvard Common Press for embracing my idea and making this book a reality.

That deep golden brown, slightly crisp surface and succulent, tender interior are the qualities of a perfectly cooked steak, chop, chicken breast, or fish fillet at a fine restaurant. How do they do it? You try at home, but the flavors just aren't as rich, the textures not quite as appealing.

What do professional chefs know that you don't?

The answer is searing.

Searing is one of the reasons that restaurant food and home cooking seem worlds apart. Learn to sear, and you too can create restaurant-quality dishes in your home kitchen. You'll have the knowledge and skill to coax the maximum flavor from each morsel of food. And perhaps the best part is that searing requires very little time, very few ingredients, and very little effort to turn out very impressive dishes. In just 15 to 20 minutes, you can put together a restaurant-caliber meal if you understand proper searing technique. And that's what *Seared to Perfection* is all about.

I realized the need for this book when I was the director and chef at In Good Taste Cooking School in Portland, Oregon. I developed and taught a popular class called Searing Mastery. But to my surprise, when I looked for a book to recommend to my students for further reading, I found nothing. I knew home cooks

needed and wanted more information, and my idea for *Seared to Perfection* grew from there.

Learning to sear is a must for meat and seafood lovers. You don't need to go to an expensive restaurant to enjoy a tender and juicy steak, chop, or fillet, and you will actually be able to achieve better results at home for a fraction of the cost.

Searing is also ideal for today's busy home cooks. It's *the* technique to keep in mind when you find yourself in the grocery store at 6:00 p.m., after work, wondering, "What's for dinner?" With its short prep and cooking times, searing is a quick, easy solution and satisfying answer.

Finally, if you consider yourself a foodie, a gourmet, or a sophisticated cook, or you simply love to entertain, knowing how to sear properly will take your cooking to the next level, allowing you to create restaurant-style dishes at home and cook spontaneously without a recipe.

what is searing?

Searing is a dry, high-heat cooking method. The result is food with a flavorful brown crust and tender interior. Searing is an ideal technique for cooking relatively thick and naturally tender foods. Beef, pork, lamb, chicken, duck, and seafood can all be seared with delectable results. Searing is also an interesting and unusual cooking method for tofu and a variety of firm fruits and vegetables. It's quick and easy; typically a food can be seared in less than five minutes per side.

The crispy crust on a properly seared food results from what is known as the Maillard browning reaction. That means when food is cooked at temperatures well above the boiling point of water, the proteins and sugars on the surface brown, and the flavors become rich and complex. Think of caramelizing sugar. White sugar is odorless and just tastes sweet, but when cooked into a caramel, it turns brown and the flavor, texture, and aroma change dramatically. The flavor of well-seared foods can be described as rich, full, savory, and satisfying.

The heat from cooking causes proteins to contract, squeezing out their juices. It has long been believed that searing "seals" in these juices, but if you watch the surface of any food as it sears, you will see that this is not true. Take a sea scallop, for example. After it hits the hot pan, moisture begins to glisten on its surface. As it continues to cook and goes from medium-rare to medium, the juices begin to pool on the surface. In fact, if the scallop is left in the pan long enough to become well-done, so much liquid is forced out that the scallop begins to simmer in its own juices—at this point it is no longer searing. So although it is true that properly seared foods are very juicy

and succulent, searing does not actually seal their surface. Seared foods are moist because they are usually served medium-rare or medium. Overcooking is what forces out juices and makes things taste dry.

Most professional chefs consider searing to be the most important cooking method because not only does it produce a delectable finished dish, but it is also the foundation of other important cooking methods. Searing is always the first step of braising and often the first step of roasting and sauce making. Searing creates rich and complex flavors that these other techniques build upon. For the best results, chunks of meat must be seared before being simmered for soup or stew, and roasts should be seared before being popped into the oven. Even for something as simple as spaghetti sauce, the ground beef and sausage are first seared until brown.

Although searing is a critical step when braising, this book is devoted solely to searing. My goals are to demonstrate that searing can stand alone as a cooking method and that it's quick and easy to do at home.

It's no accident that so many recipes instruct cooks to sear an item as the first step. The purpose is to build flavor, not obliterate any trace of pink in the food. But all too often, home cooks don't actually brown anything; they "gray" it instead! "Grayed" food looks and tastes as bland as it sounds. Knowing how to sear properly will make the dishes you cook more delicious and more flavorful, just as in the finest restaurants.

the basics of searing

selecting ingredients

Searing is an appropriate cooking method for naturally tender foods, such as steaks, chops, fillets, chicken, duck, and even tofu, vegetables, and fruits. Always select the freshest and best-quality ingredients; the dish will only be as good as what goes into it.

oil and butter

For searing, choose an oil with a relatively high smoke point (the temperature at which an oil starts to smoke and impart a burned flavor to the dish). Canola, peanut, grapeseed, light olive oil, and corn oil are all good choices. I especially like canola oil for its neutral flavor, availability, and low price. When I want to add extra flavor and richness to a dish, I use extra-virgin olive oil. Although it does have a lower smoke point, extra-virgin olive oil works beautifully for searing as long as you monitor the heat carefully. That means heating the pan correctly, working quickly to coat the bottom of the pan with the oil, and then immediately adding the food to the pan. The speedy addition of the food brings the temperature of the pan down enough to keep the oil from burning.

Butter should not be used for searing because it would burn. In these recipes, butter is used mainly to make sauces. Most recipes in the book call for unsalted butter so that you can control the salt content of the dish. Use salted butter only when specified.

salt and pepper

I prefer the clean flavor and coarse grain of kosher salt. The size of the crystals makes kosher salt convenient to pinch and sprinkle, and it is visible on the surface of the food, making it easier to gauge how much to use for seasoning. Kosher salt is inexpensive and available in supermarkets. Sea salt is also a good choice, but it is more expensive. Avoid using iodized salt, which has a harsh, metallic flavor.

Keep peppercorns in a mill and grind them as needed.

wines and spirits

Wines and liqueurs are frequently used when making sauces. When spirits are reduced, or simmered down, their flavors become more concentrated. It isn't necessary to invest in pricey wines for cooking, but do select good ones. Avoid tannic red wines, which taste harsh when reduced.

selecting cookware

A high-quality sauté pan is an absolute must for searing. The pan should be heavy enough to retain its heat when food is added, but not so heavy that it doesn't respond when the heat is decreased. Its core should be made of a very conductive material, such as aluminum or copper, for even heat distribution. The interior surface of the pan should be stainless steel so that it doesn't react with acidic ingredients and is easy to clean. An enameled cast-iron pan will also work, but its heft can make it hard to manage. (You may notice that inexpensive unlined aluminum pans are used in many restaurants. Aluminum is a very good conductor of heat, but it reacts with acidic ingredients, which can discolor sauces and impart a metallic flavor.) The handle should feel comfortable in your hand, as you will have to lift the pan to swirl the oil. Sloped sides allow easy access for flipping food with a spatula. My favorite brand of cookware is All-Clad, which combines all of these features. Poor-quality, cheap pans do not conduct heat well and have hot spots, which cause food to scorch.

The pan must also be large enough to avoid overcrowding when food is added; too much food in a pan will cause the temperature to drop. An overcrowded pan won't allow enough surface area for moisture to evaporate, and the food will sweat in its own juices and turn gray, not brown. The pan should hold all of the food in a single layer, with about an inch of space between items. I use a 12-inch skillet for recipes that call for a large pan and a 14-inch skillet for those that call for a very large pan. If you don't have a pan that big, sear the food in two batches or use two smaller pans.

Many home cooks like to use nonstick cookware, but I advise against it for searing. Nonstick pans should not be preheated to as high a temperature as regular pans because the coating can break down at high temperatures. (In fact, to prevent a nonstick pan from overheating, the cooking oil should be added to the pan before preheating.) This means that foods seared in a nonstick pan will never cook up as brown and crisp as those cooked in an uncoated pan, and there will be fewer browned bits left in the pan to enrich the sauce. And since seared food doesn't stick to a properly preheated uncoated pan, there is no need for the nonstick coating anyway. The only exception is that a heavy nonstick sauté pan can be helpful for searing delicate fish fillets.

preparing to sear

Searing, and in fact all cooking, goes much more smoothly if you take the time to prepare. In culinary-speak this is known as *mise en place,* which is French for "put in place." This means everything you need should be "in its place" before you begin to cook. It refers to mental as well as physical preparation. Read through the entire recipe once or twice to familiarize yourself with the ingredients and the procedure. Chop, slice, and measure everything before you put the pan to the heat. I even go so far as to arrange all of my ingredients by the stovetop in the order of use. Have ready a clean plate as a landing pad for the cooked food and a piece of foil for tenting it to keep it warm. You will scarcely have time to do any of this once you start cooking.

Remove all ingredients from the refrigerator about 30 minutes before you start cooking to allow them to come to room temperature. Room-temperature ingredients cook more evenly. Moisture slows the browning process, so pat the food dry with paper towels, especially if it has been soaking in a marinade.

layer—and swirl the pan to coat the bottom. Add the food immediately, without hesitation. Just a few extra seconds at this point can cause the pan to overheat and the oil to burn. If the oil thins out and coats the bottom of the pan easily, and there's a lively sizzle when the food is added to the pan, those are good indicators that the pan is hot enough.

Take care not to splatter the hot oil when you add food to the pan. For the most attractive presentation, put the food into the pan service side down—in other words, cook the top side first. The pan is clean and hot, so the side that goes into the pan first will be the prettiest, with the darkest and most even browning.

start searing

Heating the pan properly may be the most critical step in searing. To achieve a brown crust, the pan must be very hot before any food is added. Otherwise there won't be enough heat to evaporate the moisture, and the food will sweat in its own juices.

To heat a large pan, set the burner to its highest setting. If you are using a medium-size pan, setting the burner to medium may heat the pan sufficiently. The flames (on a gas burner) should hit the bottom of the pan, not lick the sides.

To test if the pan is hot enough, flick a few water droplets into it. If the water sizzles, the pan needs to be hotter. If the droplets dance on the surface and look like little ball bearings rolling around, the pan is hot enough to start searing.

Working quickly and carefully, wipe out any water droplets with a clean kitchen towel. Immediately add the oil—just enough for a thin

now leave it alone!

Many cooks fear that the food will stick, so they try to pull it away from the pan. Resist that temptation and let the food cook undisturbed. Moving the food around slows the browning process. The food will actually let you know when it's ready to be turned—it will release from the pan easily when moved with a pair of tongs or a wide fish spatula. If the food seems to be brown and ready to flip but still sticks to the pan, leave it alone. Just wait a minute longer and then check it again. Once it can be easily moved, flip the food just once using either tongs or a spatula. Most foods cook slightly longer on the first side than on the second side. And don't press down on the food with a spatula as it cooks.

Adjust the heat as necessary. Turn down the heat if the pan seems to be too hot, if the food is getting dark too quickly, or if the oil shows any sign of smoking. Add a bit of oil to the pan if at any time it looks dry.

is it done yet?

Good cooks must use all of their senses. Your first clue that the food is almost done is the aroma. Watch the sides of the food as it cooks to see how far along it is. One helpful test for doneness is to feel the firmness of the food by poking it with a finger. Foods feel soft and almost gelatinous when they are rare, and they feel firmer and firmer the longer they cook.

Some cooks use the fleshy area of their palms beneath the thumb as a doneness indicator. Bringing the thumb and first finger together simulates rare texture, the thumb to the middle finger is like medium-rare, the thumb to the fourth finger is like medium, and the thumb to the pinky finger is like well-done.

My favorite way to determine doneness, especially for steaks and chops, is to observe the amount of moisture on the surface. A rare food barely glistens. Moisture just begins to accumulate on the surface when the food is medium-rare, and juices actually start to pool when the food is cooked to medium.

Measuring internal temperature with an instant-read thermometer is the best way to tell if a larger cut, such as a tenderloin or rack of lamb, is done. Rare is about 120° to 125°F, medium-rare is 130° to 135°F, medium is 140° to 145°F, medium-well is 150° to 155°F, and well-done is 160°F. Chicken must be cooked to 165°F to be safe to eat.

searing on an electric stove

An electric stove is not nearly as responsive as a gas stove; when the heat is turned down, it takes time for the element to actually cool down. If you need to lower the heat instantly, simply pull the pan off the burner for a few seconds. This may seem awkward at first, but you will quickly find that it's the easiest and most efficient means of controlling the heat when cooking with an electric stove.

give it a rest

Once the food is removed from the pan to a plate, it will continue to cook from its residual heat. This is known as carryover cooking. Tent the food with aluminum foil to keep it warm and let it rest for several minutes. The larger the item, the longer it should rest; 5 to 10 minutes is sufficient for a steak, chop, or duck breast, but a tenderloin should rest as long as 20 minutes. Resting time is especially important for things like roasts that will be sliced because it allows them to retain their juices. If you slice a steak without letting it rest, you'll see all of those delicious juices run out onto the carving board.

making the sauce

While the food is tented and resting, make the sauce. If too much oil remains in the pan, carefully pour it off into a heatproof bowl to avoid a greasy sauce. For most sauces, there should be just enough oil in the pan to coat the bottom, about a tablespoon or less. There can be more oil, perhaps up to 2 tablespoons, for sauces or toppings that include sautéed vegetables such as onions or mushrooms.

Many sauces start with sautéed aromatics, such as garlic, shallots, or onions. Then the pan is deglazed with wine or another flavorful, and usually acidic, liquid. Deglazing means scraping up the flavorful browned bits that remain in the pan after searing with a whisk or heatproof spatula; this brown matter, known as the *fond,* the French word for "foundation," imparts a deep, rich flavor to the sauce. At this point broth, heavy cream, and flavorings may be added, and then the sauce is reduced.

Reducing means simmering until much of the liquid evaporates, the sauce thickens, and the flavors become concentrated. Traditionally, sauces are reduced until they are *nappé,* which means thick enough to coat the back of a spoon. To my eye, the sauce is thick enough when I can see the bottom of the pan as I draw the spatula through it. How thick the sauce should be is a matter of personal preference. Whisk any accumulated juices from the seared food into the sauce at this point.

For a luscious and velvety sauce, swirl in a bit of cold, unsalted butter at the end. You can use more or less butter depending on how rich you like the sauce. This technique, called *monter au beurre,* or "mounting with butter," thickens the sauce and gives it a lovely sheen. It can also balance out the flavor of a sauce that is a bit too acidic. Let the pan cool slightly before adding the butter—this will ensure that the butter doesn't separate, or break, from the sauce—and whisk quickly to combine.

seasoning "to taste"

Salt is added to food to make it taste better and bring out its inherent flavors, not to make it taste salty. Food that doesn't have enough salt tastes flat and uninteresting, so it's important to know how to season correctly. Keep in mind that you can always add more salt to a dish, but you cannot take it out once you've added too much. Add salt, a little at a time, and always taste as you go. When the flavors pop and you can taste each individual component, the dish is seasoned perfectly. If you are unsure, simply remove a small amount of the sauce to a bowl and season it. Once you think it's perfect, add a little more salt and taste again. Does it taste better now, or is it just too salty? Now you have trained your palate, and you know exactly how it should taste. Return this small amount to the rest of the sauce and season the entire quantity.

slicing against the grain

Large roasts and birds and certain cuts with long muscle fibers, such as flank and hanger steaks, must be carved before being served. Once the food has rested, thinly slice it against the grain.

serve immediately

Arrange the seared food on individual plates or a serving platter. For a restaurant-style presentation, fan out sliced foods decoratively. Pour the sauce all over the seared food, or transfer it to a gravy boat and pass it at the table. I also like to pass a tiny bowl of coarse sea salt, such as *fleur de sel,* for diners to sprinkle on as desired. The crunch and extra salty zing are the perfect finishing touches.

cleaning up

Oil vaporizes during searing, so keep the stove vent operating on its highest setting for the duration of the cooking time. I also use a splatter screen to keep down the mess. And forget elbow grease—the easiest way to clean cooked-on residue from a pan is to deglaze it with water. Add about a cup of water to the pan, bring it to a boil over high heat, and scrape up any bits from the bottom of the pan with a heatproof spatula—they will come off effortlessly. Then let the pan cool and rinse it with soap and water. Use an all-purpose cleaner to remove oil spattered on the stovetop.

scaling the recipes

To cut any of the searing recipes in half, use a medium-size pan—a 10-inch pan would be about right. To double a recipe, sear the food in two or more batches, or use two pans and then make a single large batch of sauce. The doubled quantity of sauce will have to simmer longer to become thick.

make the technique your own

You'll notice that the procedures for most of the recipes are very similar. Try just a few of them, and you'll quickly get the hang of searing technique. Once you understand the method, you'll be able to mix and match any meat, poultry, or seafood item with any sauce in the book, and eventually you will be able to improvise and create your own recipes.

beef

> "When it comes to a steak, fat is your friend. Select well-marbled steaks with flecks of fat throughout the meat."

A big juicy steak is quite possibly the single most satisfying entrée you can serve. For the perfect seared steak, you must start with the right cut of meat: Sirloin, New York strip, rib-eye, flatiron, flank, hanger, tenderloin, and T-bone steaks are all tender cuts of meat and therefore good choices for searing.

When it comes to a steak, fat is your friend. Select well-marbled steaks with flecks of fat throughout the meat. This fat will baste the meat as it cooks, keeping it moist, juicy, and flavorful. Prime-grade beef has, by far, the most marbling but is quite expensive and difficult to find at the retail level. Choice-grade beef is well marbled, relatively affordable, and readily available in gourmet markets. Select and lesser grades of beef have little to no marbling.

For the recipes in this book, select your steaks by thickness, not weight. It is the thickness of the steak that determines how long it should cook, and weights are listed in the recipes only as a guide for portion size. For example, a 10-ounce rib-eye steak and a 14-ounce rib-eye steak of the same thickness will take the same amount of time to cook. Select the steak that suits your appetite. If you and your guests have small appetites, or if the dish is being served as a part of a multicourse meal, you can cut each steak in half crosswise before cooking.

Most chefs agree that beef steaks are best served medium-rare. A rare steak is barely warm all the way through and has a soft, mushy center. A medium-rare steak is heated enough to actually melt the marbled fat, releasing the most flavor. The center of a medium-rare steak is warm, tender, yielding but with a good chew, and juicy. Steaks cooked to medium, medium-well, or well-done are progressively tougher and drier because continued heat forces more and more moisture out of the meat. If you do prefer your steaks cooked to medium or beyond, sear them according to the recipe and finish them in a hot oven, as if you were cooking chicken breasts (page 58).

- **Sirloin steaks:** The sirloin is cut from the rear end of the loin. These steaks have a bold, beefy flavor. They are tender but less so than any of the other steaks listed here, so they're easy on the budget.

- **New York strip steaks:** New York strips come from the loin. They are very tender and have a robust flavor. They're a favorite of steak lovers.

- **Rib-eye steaks:** These come from the rib and are the same cut as prime rib. They have plenty of luscious fat and flavor. Rib-eye steaks are frequently the choice of steak connoisseurs, and they also happen to be my very favorite.

- **Flatiron steaks:** Flatiron steaks are extremely tender, second only to the tenderloin. These steaks are quite succulent and have a very bold, almost livery flavor. They are relatively unknown to home cooks, so they're still quite affordable.

- **Flank steaks:** The flank steak comes from the belly of the steer. It has loads of flavor and a pleasant chew. Long muscle fibers run its length, so this steak must be cut against the grain into very thin slices for serving.

- **Hanger steaks:** The hanger steak is a tender cut of meat and has a very bold flavor, much like the flatiron steak. It's delicious and quite a bargain when compared to other steaks. The hanger steak should be sliced against the grain for serving.

- **Tenderloin steaks:** Of all of the cuts of beef, tenderloin steaks are the most tender and, at the same time, the most delicately flavored. They are also the most expensive, by far.

- **T-bone steaks:** Also known as porterhouse steaks, T-bones are part New York strip and part tenderloin. They are good for searing, but when the meat contracts as it cooks, the bone can keep it from making good contact with the pan.

the perfect burger

Whether it's seared in a pan or on a grill, the perfect burger should have a crunchy crust, juicy center, pronounced beef flavor, and good bun coverage. So what's the secret? The meat. Choose ground round or ground chuck with enough fat to keep it moist. Lean ground beef such as sirloin yields a dry, flavorless burger. For tender burgers, handle the beef as little as possible; do not overwork it. If your hamburgers cook up as thick as they are wide and cover only half of the bun, keep in mind that meat contracts as it cooks. When shaping patties, make them thinner in the center than around the edges and slightly larger than the bun. Cook the burgers over medium-high heat, and don't press down on the patties with a spatula or all of their precious juices will be lost. Finally, serve the burgers on hearty bakery-style buns or Kaiser rolls, not wimpy grocery store buns.

Serves 4

2 pounds ground beef containing no less than 16 percent fat

Kosher salt and freshly ground black pepper

2 tablespoons canola oil

4 hearty hamburger buns, split

Garnishes as desired: lettuce, tomato, raw or caramelized onions (page 21), pickles, cheese, bacon, jalapeño chiles, mayonnaise, mustard, and/or ketchup

Divide the ground beef into 4 equal portions and gently form each portion into a ball. Gently pat each ball into the shape of a hamburger patty about 4½ inches across, slightly thinner in the center and thicker around the edges. Season the patties generously with salt and pepper and set aside at room temperature for about 30 minutes.

Heat a large, heavy sauté pan over medium-high heat until very hot but not smoking. Add the oil and swirl to coat the bottom of the pan. Add the patties and cook without disturbing for 4 to 5 minutes, or until they release from the pan and are crusty and brown. Using a spatula, turn the patties over and continue to cook over medium-high heat for another 3 to 4 minutes, or until they reach the desired doneness. Moisture will pool on the surface of the patties and they will be firm to the touch when they are medium-well. Remove the patties to a plate, tent with foil to keep warm, and allow to rest for 5 minutes.

Meanwhile, toast the buns, if desired. Serve the patties on the buns immediately, topped with the desired garnishes.

blue cheese burgers

You can create endless variations on this recipe, substituting different cheeses, such as pepper Jack or cheddar, or even a compound butter (pages 32–33), such as one with thyme and roasted garlic, for the blue cheese.

Serves 4

Divide the ground beef into 8 equal portions and gently form each portion into a ball. Gently pat each ball into the shape of a hamburger patty about 4½ inches across, slightly thinner in the center and thicker around the edges. Spread 2 tablespoons of the blue cheese crumbles over each of 4 patties and top with the remaining 4 patties, pressing so that they adhere. Season the patties generously with salt and pepper and set aside at room temperature for about 30 minutes.

Heat a large, heavy sauté pan over medium-high heat until very hot but not smoking. Add the oil and swirl to coat the bottom of the pan. Add the patties and cook without disturbing for 4 to 5 minutes, or until they release from the pan and are crusty and brown. Using a spatula, turn the patties over and continue to cook over medium-high heat for another 3 to 4 minutes, or until they reach the desired doneness. Moisture will pool on the surface of the patties and they will be firm to the touch when they are medium-well. Remove the patties to a plate, tent with foil to keep warm, and allow to rest for 5 minutes.

Meanwhile, toast the buns, if desired. Serve the patties on the buns immediately, topped with the caramelized onions.

2 pounds ground beef containing no less than 16 percent fat

½ cup crumbled blue cheese

Kosher salt and freshly ground black pepper

2 tablespoons canola oil

4 hearty hamburger buns, split

½ cup caramelized onions (page 21)

lavender-peppercorn steaks with horseradish sauce

The combination of beef and lavender is both unusual and magical—the bold floral fragrance of the herb permeates the meat as it sears. Look for edible, culinary-grade lavender in the spice section of gourmet markets.

Serves 4

Four 1- to 1¼-inch-thick sirloin steaks, weighing about 10 ounces each

Kosher salt

4 ounces cream cheese, softened

¼ cup prepared horseradish

2 tablespoons mayonnaise

2 tablespoons Dijon mustard

2 tablespoons freshly cracked black peppercorns

1 tablespoon dried lavender flowers

2 tablespoons extra-virgin olive oil

Season the steaks generously with salt and set aside at room temperature for about 30 minutes. To make the sauce, blend the cream cheese, horseradish, mayonnaise, and mustard in a medium-size bowl.

Combine the peppercorns and lavender in a small bowl. Coat the steaks with the lavender and pepper blend, pressing it gently into the meat. Heat a large, heavy sauté pan over high heat until very hot but not smoking. Add the oil and swirl to coat the bottom of the pan. Add the steaks and cook without disturbing for 4 to 5 minutes, or until they release from the pan and are crusty and brown. Using tongs, turn the steaks over and continue to cook over high heat for another 2 to 3 minutes, or until they reach the desired doneness. Moisture will just begin to accumulate on the surface of the steaks when they are medium-rare. Remove the steaks to a plate, tent with foil to keep warm, and allow to rest for 5 minutes.

Arrange the steaks on individual plates, divide the sauce among the steaks, and serve immediately.

steaks with pepper relish

The pepper relish can be made up to two days ahead and kept refrigerated in a tightly sealed container, but let it come to room temperature before serving. It's also delicious served over seared fish fillets. If you are not familiar with the technique of julienne, see the tutorial on my blog, Hungry Cravings (http://hungrycravings.com).   Serves 4

Season the steaks generously with salt and pepper and set aside at room temperature for about 30 minutes. To make the relish, combine the bell peppers, chile, garlic, vinegar, and brown sugar in a medium-size bowl. Season with salt to taste.

Heat a large, heavy sauté pan over high heat until very hot but not smoking. Add the oil and swirl to coat the bottom of the pan. Add the steaks and cook without disturbing for 4 to 5 minutes, or until they release from the pan and are crusty and brown. Using tongs, turn the steaks over and continue to cook over high heat for another 2 to 3 minutes, or until they reach the desired doneness. Moisture will just begin to accumulate on the surface of the steaks when they are medium-rare. Remove the steaks to a plate, tent with foil to keep warm, and allow to rest for 5 minutes.

Arrange the steaks on individual plates, divide the relish among the steaks, and serve immediately.

Four 1- to 1¼-inch-thick sirloin steaks, weighing about 10 ounces each

Kosher salt and freshly ground black pepper

1 roasted red bell pepper (page 92), julienned

1 roasted yellow bell pepper (page 92), julienned

1 roasted Anaheim or poblano chile (page 92), julienned

1 clove garlic, minced

1 tablespoon cider vinegar

1 tablespoon light brown sugar

2 tablespoons extra-virgin olive oil

new york steaks
with boursin sauce

Boursin is a mild, creamy cheese that is widely available in supermarkets. The flavored varieties, such as garlic and herb or black pepper, make for quick sauces, with no mincing of garlic, shallots, or herbs required.

Serves 4

Four 1- to 1¼-inch-thick strip steaks, weighing about 12 ounces each

Kosher salt and freshly ground black pepper

2 tablespoons extra-virgin olive oil

2 tablespoons white wine

½ cup heavy cream

One 5.2-ounce package flavored Boursin cheese, crumbled

Season the steaks generously with salt and pepper and set aside at room temperature for about 30 minutes.

Heat a large, heavy sauté pan over high heat until very hot but not smoking. Add the oil and swirl to coat the bottom of the pan. Add the steaks and cook without disturbing for 4 to 5 minutes, or until they release from the pan and are crusty and brown. Using tongs, turn the steaks over and continue to cook over high heat for another 2 to 3 minutes, or until they reach the desired doneness. Moisture will just begin to accumulate on the surface of the steaks when they are medium-rare. Remove the steaks to a plate and tent with foil to keep warm.

Reduce the heat to medium, add the wine to the pan, and simmer for a minute or so, scraping up the browned bits from the bottom of the pan with a heatproof spatula. Add the cream and simmer for another 1 to 2 minutes, or until the sauce is slightly thickened. Remove the pan from the heat and let cool for a minute or two. Whisk in the Boursin, stir in any accumulated juices from the steaks, and season with salt and pepper to taste.

Arrange the steaks on individual plates, divide the sauce among the steaks, and serve immediately.

new york steaks with gorgonzola sauce

Steak and blue cheese is a classic flavor combination. I use Gorgonzola dolce, which is a mild and sweet variety of Gorgonzola, for this sauce, but any type of blue cheese will do.

Follow the recipe for New York Steaks with Boursin Sauce, substituting 1¼ cups crumbled Gorgonzola cheese for the Boursin. Finish the sauce by adding 2 tablespoons minced fresh chives.

strip steaks with shallots

Sautéing shallots in butter mellows their pungent onion flavor and brings out their natural sweetness. Cook the shallots slowly until they are translucent and tender, but do not allow them to brown. If you do see any signs of color, turn down the heat slightly.

Serves 4

Four 1- to 1¼-inch-thick strip steaks, weighing about 12 ounces each

Kosher salt and freshly ground black pepper

2 tablespoons extra-virgin olive oil

2 tablespoons unsalted butter

1 cup minced shallots

1 teaspoon minced fresh thyme

1 teaspoon minced Italian parsley (optional)

Season the steaks generously with salt and pepper and set aside at room temperature for about 30 minutes.

Heat a large, heavy sauté pan over high heat until very hot but not smoking. Add the oil and swirl to coat the bottom of the pan. Add the steaks and cook without disturbing for 4 to 5 minutes, or until they release from the pan and are crusty and brown. Using tongs, turn the steaks over and continue to cook over high heat for another 2 to 3 minutes, or until they reach the desired doneness. Moisture will just begin to accumulate on the surface of the steaks when they are medium-rare. Remove the steaks to a plate and tent with foil to keep warm.

Reduce the heat to medium-low, add the butter and shallots to the pan, and sauté for 2 to 3 minutes, or until the shallots are translucent and soft. Stir in the thyme, parsley (if using), and any accumulated juices from the steaks and season with salt and pepper to taste.

Arrange the steaks on individual plates, divide the shallot mixture among the steaks, and serve immediately.

steak au poivre
with red wine sauce

No bistro menu would be complete without steak au poivre, the classic French dish of tender steak encrusted with crushed black peppercorns. Although the recipe calls for what seems like an enormous amount of pepper, high heat works an amazing transformation on the pungent spice—the peppercorns become toasted and mellow. For this dish, the peppercorns should be coarsely crushed, not ground to a powder. Crack whole black peppercorns with a spice mill or in a mortar and pestle. Alternatively, place them in a zipper-top plastic bag and tap them with a rolling pin or the bottom of a small frying pan.   Serves 4

Season the steaks generously with salt and set aside at room temperature for about 30 minutes.

Coat the steaks with the peppercorns, pressing them gently into the meat. Heat a large, heavy sauté pan over high heat until very hot but not smoking. Add the oil and swirl to coat the bottom of the pan. Add the steaks and cook without disturbing for 4 to 5 minutes, or until they release from the pan and are crusty and brown. Using tongs, turn the steaks over and continue to cook over high heat for another 2 to 3 minutes, or until they reach the desired doneness. Moisture will just begin to accumulate on the surface of the steaks when they are medium-rare. Remove the steaks to a plate and tent with foil to keep warm.

Reduce the heat to medium, add the shallot to the pan, and sauté for 30 seconds, or until translucent and fragrant. Add the wine and simmer for a minute or so, scraping up the browned bits from the bottom of the pan with a heatproof spatula. Add the broth and thyme and simmer for another 5 to 6 minutes, or until the sauce is thickened. Remove the pan from the heat, discard the thyme, and let the sauce cool for a minute or two. Whisk in the butter quickly, stir in any accumulated juices from the steaks, and season with salt to taste.

Arrange the steaks on individual plates, divide the sauce among the steaks, and serve immediately.

Four 1- to 1¼-inch-thick strip or rib-eye steaks, weighing about 12 ounces each

Kosher salt

2 tablespoons freshly cracked black peppercorns

2 tablespoons extra-virgin olive oil

1 shallot, minced

½ cup red wine

½ cup beef broth

2 sprigs fresh thyme

2 to 3 tablespoons cold unsalted butter, diced, to your taste

steak tataki

If you frequent Japanese restaurants, you may be familiar with *tataki,* a dish of beef or fish (such as tuna or salmon) that is seared rare, cooled, and then marinated. It's perfect for summer entertaining because it is light and delicious, and the cooking is done the day before the dish is to be served. If you are not familiar with the technique of julienne, see the tutorial on my blog, Hungry Cravings (http://hungrycravings.com). Kelp and bonito flakes are available at Asian markets. I serve Steak Tataki with a side of sushi rice or plain sticky rice.

Serves 4

Three 1- to 1¼-inch-thick strip steaks, weighing about 12 ounces each, trimmed of any fat and gristle

Kosher salt and freshly ground black pepper

¼ cup sake

¼ cup soy sauce

2 tablespoons sugar

1 tablespoon unseasoned rice vinegar

1 tablespoon freshly squeezed lime juice

2 slices fresh ginger, julienned

One 2-inch-square piece kelp

½ cup bonito flakes

Several drops of dark sesame oil, to your taste

2 tablespoons canola oil

1 cup julienned yellow onion

1 cup julienned daikon

1 cup julienned carrot

1 tablespoon sesame seeds, toasted

Season the steaks generously with salt and pepper and set aside at room temperature for about 30 minutes.

Combine the sake, soy sauce, sugar, vinegar, lime juice, ginger, and kelp in a small saucepan. Bring to a boil and simmer for 2 to 3 minutes, or until the kelp is rehydrated. Remove from the heat, add the bonito flakes and sesame oil, and let stand for 2 to 3 minutes, or until the bonito flakes are rehydrated and sink to the bottom. Strain the mixture through a fine-mesh sieve into a bowl, let cool, and transfer to a large zipper-top plastic bag.

Heat a large, heavy sauté pan over high heat until very hot but not smoking. Add the canola oil and swirl to coat the bottom of the pan. Add the steaks and cook without disturbing for 2 to 3 minutes, or until they release from the pan and are crusty and brown. Using tongs, turn the steaks over and continue to cook over high heat for another 1 to 2 minutes, or until they are rare. The steaks will be soft to the touch. Remove the steaks to a plate and let cool.

Add the steaks to the marinade in the zipper-top plastic bag and turn to coat. Seal the bag, letting out all the air. Marinate the steaks overnight in the refrigerator.

Remove the steaks from the marinade, reserving the marinade. Slice the steaks thinly against the grain. Toss the onion, daikon, and carrot with the reserved marinade in a medium-size bowl.

Spoon a portion of the vegetable mixture into the center of each of four plates. Arrange the steak slices atop each mound of vegetables and sprinkle with the sesame seeds. Serve immediately.

rib-eye steaks
with caramelized onions

Although this recipe calls for two separate sauté pans, you can get by with just one. Caramelize the onions first, clean the pan, and then sear the steaks in the same pan.   **Serves 4**

Four 1- to 1¼-inch-thick
rib-eye steaks, weighing
about 12 ounces each

Kosher salt and freshly ground
black pepper

¼ cup (½ stick) unsalted
butter

2 large yellow onions,
julienned

2 tablespoons extra-virgin
olive oil

2 tablespoons red wine

½ teaspoon minced
fresh thyme

Season the steaks generously with salt and pepper and set aside at room temperature for about 30 minutes. Meanwhile, heat a large, heavy sauté pan over medium-low heat. Add the butter and onions and cook, stirring frequently, for 30 to 35 minutes, or until caramelized.

When the onions are nearly done, heat another large, heavy sauté pan over high heat until very hot but not smoking. Add the oil and swirl to coat the bottom of the pan. Add the steaks and cook without disturbing for 4 to 5 minutes, or until they release from the pan and are crusty and brown. Using tongs, turn the steaks over and continue to cook over high heat for another 2 to 3 minutes, or until they reach the desired doneness. Moisture will just begin to accumulate on the surface of the steaks when they are medium-rare. Remove the steaks to a plate and tent with foil to keep warm.

Reduce the heat to medium, add the wine and thyme to the pan, and simmer for a minute or so, scraping up the browned bits from the bottom of the pan with a heatproof spatula. Stir in the caramelized onions and any accumulated juices from the steaks and season with salt and pepper to taste.

Arrange the steaks on individual plates, divide the caramelized onions among the steaks, and serve immediately.

caramelized onions

Caramelized onions add so much flavor to so many different foods, from seared steaks to burgers and sandwiches to vegetable and grain dishes. As they cook, the onions slowly turn a deep brown and become sweet and meltingly tender.

For the best results, choose yellow or sweet onions. Cut the onions into uniform julienne pieces for even cooking. Do not slice the onions into rounds or half-moons because the small pieces from the center of the onion will burn before the largest pieces brown. (See my blog, Hungry Cravings, http://hungrycravings.com, for a demonstration of how to julienne an onion—it's not the same as slicing it!) And keep in mind that what seems like a huge heap of raw onions will cook down considerably. One medium-size onion yields about ½ cup caramelized onions. Cook the onions in an ample amount of oil and/or butter, about 2 tablespoons per onion, in a large, heavy pan over low to medium-low heat for 30 to 35 minutes, stirring often. You should hear a soft, slow sizzle for the duration of the cooking time. If you hear a lively sizzle, as in sautéing, turn the heat down slightly—the onions will burn before they caramelize if the heat is too high. At first the onions will exude moisture, as if they're sweating. Once most of the moisture evaporates, they will begin to brown. The color and flavor take time to develop; properly caramelized onions take at least 30 minutes to make. Caramelized onions can be prepared up to several days in advance and kept tightly sealed in the refrigerator.

chile-lime marinated rib-eye steaks

The flavors of the Southwest inspire this bold marinade. Plan ahead when making this recipe because the steaks benefit from being marinated overnight. Mango Salsa (page 88) is a fine accompaniment.

Serves 4

2 tablespoons freshly squeezed lime juice

2 tablespoons soy sauce

1 tablespoon honey

2 tablespoons Worcestershire sauce

2 cloves garlic, minced

3 tablespoons pure chile powder

Four 1- to 1¼-inch-thick rib-eye steaks, weighing about 12 ounces each

2 tablespoons canola oil

Combine the lime juice, soy sauce, honey, Worcestershire sauce, garlic, and chile powder in a large zipper-top plastic bag. Add the steaks and turn to coat. Seal the bag, letting out all the air. Marinate the steaks for at least 2 hours, or up to 24 hours, in the refrigerator.

Remove the steaks from the marinade and set aside at room temperature for about 30 minutes. Discard the marinade.

Pat the steaks dry with paper towels. Heat a large, heavy sauté pan over medium-high heat until very hot but not smoking. Add the oil and swirl to coat the bottom of the pan. Add the steaks and cook without disturbing for 4 to 5 minutes, or until they release from the pan and are crusty and brown. Using tongs, turn the steaks over and continue to cook over medium-high heat for another 2 to 3 minutes, or until they reach the desired doneness. Moisture will just begin to accumulate on the surface of the steaks when they are medium-rare. Remove the steaks to a plate, tent with foil to keep warm, and allow to rest for 5 minutes.

Arrange the steaks on individual plates and serve immediately.

chile powder

For the brightest and most intense chile flavor, select a pure chile powder, such as ancho or pasilla, rather than a blend, which often includes cumin, garlic, oregano, and other spices. And don't be afraid to use lots of it—powdered chiles, although very flavorful, are not very hot. Most gourmet markets carry pure chile powders.

rib-eye steaks
with soy-butter sauce

This simple dish combines seared steaks and soy sauce for a big umami punch. Try these steaks with Steamed Baby Bok Choy (page 141) and a side of sticky rice. Serves 4

Season the steaks generously with salt and pepper and set aside at room temperature for about 30 minutes.

Heat a large, heavy sauté pan over high heat until very hot but not smoking. Add the oil and swirl to coat the bottom of the pan. Add the steaks and cook without disturbing for 4 to 5 minutes, or until they release from the pan and are crusty and brown. Using tongs, turn the steaks over and continue to cook over high heat for another 2 to 3 minutes, or until they reach the desired doneness. Moisture will just begin to accumulate on the surface of the steaks when they are medium-rare. Remove the steaks to a plate and tent with foil to keep warm.

Reduce the heat to medium, add the garlic to the pan, and sauté for 30 seconds, or until fragrant. Add the soy sauce and simmer for a minute or so, scraping up the browned bits from the bottom of the pan with a heatproof spatula. Remove the pan from the heat and let cool for a minute or two. Whisk in the butter quickly, stir in any accumulated juices from the steaks, and season with pepper to taste.

Arrange the steaks on individual plates, divide the sauce among the steaks, and serve immediately.

Four 1- to 1¼-inch-thick rib-eye steaks, weighing about 12 ounces each

Kosher salt and freshly ground black pepper

2 tablespoons extra-virgin olive oil

1 clove garlic, minced

¼ cup soy sauce

½ cup (1 stick) cold unsalted butter, diced

umami

The taste buds on the human tongue can detect five basic tastes—sweet, sour, salty, bitter, and umami. Sure, you know the first four, but have you heard of umami? You most certainly have tasted it. Steaks, Parmigiano-Reggiano cheese, shiitake mushrooms, seaweed, soy sauce, fish sauce, Worcestershire sauce, ketchup, and red wine are just a few examples of umami foods. Umami can be described as savory, brothy, mouth-filling, rich, meaty, hearty, or satisfying. Searing brings out the umami taste in foods, and using two or more umami ingredients together in a single dish results in an umami taste explosion, creating a dish in which the whole is far greater than the sum of its parts. That's why a simple recipe like Rib-Eye Steaks with Soy-Butter Sauce can taste so complex.

steaks with chipotle cream sauce

Dried Mexican oregano, which has a unique floral character, can be found at some gourmet grocers and (usually for less than a dollar) at Mexican markets. If you cannot find it, just omit it from the recipe; do not substitute common oregano. Canned chipotle chiles in adobo sauce are available at most supermarkets. If you prefer a mild sauce, or if you are unsure of how many chipotles to use, start with just one or two. Taste the sauce after you puree it. You can always add more chipotles to the blender if you want to increase the heat. Don't worry about the seeds as they will be removed when the sauce is strained. Leftover chiles keep well frozen. Serve these steaks with Baked Sweet Potatoes (page 135).   Serves 4

Four 1- to 1¼-inch-thick rib-eye steaks, weighing about 12 ounces each

Kosher salt and freshly ground black pepper

2 tablespoons canola oil

¼ cup diced yellow onion

1 clove garlic, minced

¼ teaspoon ground cumin

Pinch of Mexican oregano

¼ cup beer, preferably Mexican or pale ale

½ cup chicken broth

½ cup heavy cream

2 to 3 chipotle chiles in adobo sauce, minced, to your taste

1 teaspoon freshly squeezed lime juice

Season the steaks generously with salt and pepper and set aside at room temperature for about 30 minutes.

Heat a large, heavy sauté pan over high heat until very hot but not smoking. Add the oil and swirl to coat the bottom of the pan. Add the steaks and cook without disturbing for 4 to 5 minutes, or until they release from the pan and are crusty and brown. Using tongs, turn the steaks over and continue to cook over high heat for another 2 to 3 minutes, or until they reach the desired doneness. Moisture will just begin to accumulate on the surface of the steaks when they are medium-rare. Remove the steaks to a plate and tent with foil to keep warm.

Reduce the heat to medium; add the onion, garlic, and a generous pinch of salt to the pan. Sauté for 1 to 2 minutes, or until the onion and garlic are soft. Stir in the cumin and oregano. Add the beer and simmer for a minute or so, scraping up the browned bits from the bottom of the pan with a heatproof spatula. Add the broth, cream, and chipotles and simmer for another 4 to 5 minutes, or until the sauce is thickened. Carefully transfer the sauce to a blender and blend until smooth. Strain the sauce through a fine-mesh sieve back into the sauté pan and reheat. Stir in the lime juice and any accumulated juices from the steaks and season with salt to taste.

Arrange the steaks on individual plates, divide the sauce among the steaks, and serve immediately.

flatiron steaks
with sautéed mushrooms

Flatiron steaks, also known as top blade steaks, are largely unknown to home cooks but are quite popular in restaurants. Flatirons come from the chuck or shoulder and are very tender with a bold, beefy flavor. In fact, flatiron steaks are the second most tender cut of beef after the tenderloin, but they are much more affordable. Most butcher shops and gourmet grocers carry them. Mushrooms and shallots sautéed in sweet butter are a traditional accompaniment to a succulent steak. Choose a combination of cultivated button, cremini, and shiitake mushrooms. For a special occasion, splurge on some seasonal wild mushrooms such as chanterelles in the fall or spring morels. Serves 4

Season the steaks generously with salt and pepper and set aside at room temperature for about 30 minutes.

Heat a large, heavy sauté pan over high heat until very hot but not smoking. Add the oil and swirl to coat the bottom of the pan. Add the steaks and cook without disturbing for 3 to 4 minutes, or until they release from the pan and are crusty and brown. Using tongs, turn the steaks over and continue to cook over high heat for another 2 to 3 minutes, or until they reach the desired doneness. Moisture will just begin to accumulate on the surface of the steaks when they are medium-rare. Remove the steaks to a plate and tent with foil to keep warm.

Reduce the heat to medium, add the shallots to the pan, and sauté for 30 seconds, or until translucent and fragrant. Add the butter, mushrooms, and thyme (if using) and sauté for another 5 to 6 minutes, or until the mushrooms are soft. Add the wine and simmer for a minute or so, scraping up the browned bits from the bottom of the pan with a heatproof spatula. Stir in any accumulated juices from the steaks and season with salt and pepper to taste.

Arrange the steaks on individual plates, divide the mushroom mixture among the steaks, and serve immediately.

4 flatiron steaks, weighing about 8 ounces each

Kosher salt and freshly ground black pepper

2 tablespoons extra-virgin olive oil

2 shallots, minced

1 tablespoon unsalted butter

12 ounces mushrooms, sliced

1 teaspoon minced fresh thyme (optional)

1 tablespoon red wine

hanger steaks
with shiitake sauce

The little-known hanger steak, also called the hanging tender or *onglet* in French, comes from the diaphragm of the steer. Long and thin, it has a slight livery flavor and is juicy and tender when cooked medium-rare and sliced against the grain. And it happens to be roughly half the price of more popular steaks such as rib-eyes and New York strips. Ask your butcher for thick, even steaks, as hanging tenders vary in size and can taper at one end. They are somewhat triangular in shape, so be sure to sear them on all three sides, starting with the broadest side and ending with the narrowest. Dried and rehydrated shiitake mushrooms have a more concentrated flavor than fresh, making them the perfect accompaniment to steaks. They are available in supermarkets as well as Asian and other specialty stores.

Serves 4 to 6

3 hanger steaks, weighing about 12 ounces each

Kosher salt and freshly ground black pepper

8 dried shiitake mushrooms

1 cup hot water

1 tablespoon cornstarch

1 tablespoon water

2 tablespoons canola oil

2 cloves garlic, minced

2 tablespoons sake

½ cup beef broth

1 tablespoon soy sauce

Season the steaks generously with salt and pepper and set aside at room temperature for about 30 minutes.

Combine the shiitakes and hot water in a small bowl and let soak for 10 to 12 minutes, or until rehydrated and pliable. Remove the shiitakes to a cutting board, trim off and discard the stems, and thinly slice the caps. Strain the soaking liquid through a fine-mesh sieve into a bowl and reserve. Whisk together the cornstarch and water in a small bowl.

Heat a large, heavy sauté pan over high heat until very hot but not smoking. Add the oil and swirl to coat the bottom of the pan. Add the steaks, broad side down, and cook without disturbing for 4 to 5 minutes, or until they release from the pan and are crusty and brown. Using tongs, turn the steaks onto another side and cook for 2 to 3 minutes more. Turn the steaks onto the third side and continue to cook over high heat for another 1 to 2 minutes, or until they reach the desired doneness. Moisture will just begin to accumulate on the surface of the steaks when they are medium-rare. Remove the steaks to a plate and tent with foil to keep warm.

Reduce the heat to medium, add the garlic to the pan, and sauté for 30 seconds, or until fragrant. Add the sake and simmer for a minute or so, scraping up the browned bits from the bottom of the pan with a heatproof spatula. Add the broth, soy sauce, mushrooms, and mushroom soaking liquid and bring to a boil. Stir the cornstarch mixture to recombine and whisk it into the sauce. Simmer for another minute, or until the sauce is thickened. Stir in any accumulated juices from the steaks and season with pepper to taste.

Slice the steaks thinly against the grain. Arrange the slices on individual plates, divide the sauce among the steaks, and serve immediately.

sherry-garlic flank steak

Flank steak is an inexpensive cut of meat, ideal for serving to a crowd. Although it is more fibrous than pricier steaks, it is quite tender when cooked to medium-rare and cut against the grain into very thin slices. This marinated steak, with the flavor of sherry shining through, is tasty served hot, but it can also be served warm or even chilled over lightly dressed salad greens; the steak elevates a salad from simple to spectacular. Make steak sandwiches with the leftovers.   Serves 4

2 tablespoons sherry

2 tablespoons soy sauce

2 tablespoons honey

2 cloves garlic, minced

Generous pinch of red pepper flakes, to your taste

Freshly ground black pepper

1 flank steak, weighing 1 to 1½ pounds

2 tablespoons canola oil

Combine the sherry, soy sauce, honey, garlic, red pepper flakes, and black pepper to taste in a large zipper-top plastic bag. Add the steak and turn to coat. Seal the bag, letting out all the air. Marinate the steak for at least 2 hours, or up to 24 hours, in the refrigerator.

Remove the steak from the marinade and set aside at room temperature for about 30 minutes. Discard the marinade.

Pat the steak dry with paper towels. Heat a large, heavy sauté pan over medium-high heat until very hot but not smoking. Add the oil and swirl to coat the bottom of the pan. Add the steak and cook without disturbing for 3 to 4 minutes, or until it releases from the pan and is crusty and brown. Using tongs, turn the steak over and continue to cook over medium-high heat for another 3 to 4 minutes, or until it reaches the desired doneness. Moisture will just begin to accumulate on the surface of the steak when it is medium-rare. Remove the steak to a plate, tent with foil to keep warm, and allow to rest for 8 to 10 minutes.

Slice the steak thinly against the grain. Arrange the slices on individual plates and serve immediately.

seared fillets of beef with port reduction sauce

A dinner of seared beef tenderloin steaks is a simple luxury, perfect for easy entertaining or a romantic evening. Add this slightly sweet and velvety port sauce to your repertoire; it accents any red meat such as seared lamb chops or seared duck breasts beautifully. I serve this dish with a seasonal vegetable and Potato Gratin (page 133) and pretend I'm dining in a Parisian bistro.

Serves 4

Season the steaks generously with salt and pepper and set aside at room temperature for about 30 minutes.

Heat a large, heavy sauté pan over high heat until very hot but not smoking. Add the oil and swirl to coat the bottom of the pan. Add the steaks and cook without disturbing for 4 to 5 minutes, or until they release from the pan and are crusty and brown. Using tongs, turn the steaks over and continue to cook over high heat for another 3 to 4 minutes, or until they reach the desired doneness. Moisture will just begin to accumulate on the surface of the steaks when they are medium-rare. Remove the steaks to a plate and tent with foil to keep warm.

Reduce the heat to medium, add the shallot to the pan, and sauté for 30 seconds, or until translucent and fragrant. Add the port and thyme and simmer, scraping up the browned bits from the bottom of the pan with a heatproof spatula, for 4 to 5 minutes, or until the sauce is thickened and slightly syrupy. Remove the pan from the heat, discard the thyme, and let cool for a minute or two. Whisk in the butter quickly, stir in any accumulated juices from the steaks, and season with salt and pepper to taste.

Arrange the steaks on individual plates, divide the sauce among the steaks, and serve immediately.

Four 1¼- to 1½-inch-thick beef tenderloin steaks, weighing about 8 ounces each

Kosher salt and freshly ground black pepper

2 tablespoons extra-virgin olive oil

1 shallot, minced

1 cup ruby port

2 sprigs fresh thyme

2 to 3 tablespoons cold unsalted butter, diced, to your taste

tenderloin steaks with garlic butter

Nothing enhances the flavor of a beef tenderloin steak like the sweetness of butter and the pungency of garlic. The tenderloin is cut from the loin. It comes from the least exercised muscle in the steer, so, as the name implies, it's the single most tender cut of meat and also the most mildly flavored. It's relatively lean, so flavored butters or cream sauces are the best accompaniments.

Serves 4

Four 1¼- to 1½-inch-thick beef tenderloin steaks, weighing about 8 ounces each

Kosher salt and freshly ground black pepper

¼ cup (½ stick) salted butter, softened

1½ teaspoons minced garlic

2 tablespoons extra-virgin olive oil

Season the steaks generously with salt and pepper and set aside at room temperature for about 30 minutes. Blend the butter and garlic in a medium-size bowl.

Heat a large, heavy sauté pan over high heat until very hot but not smoking. Add the oil and swirl to coat the bottom of the pan. Add the steaks and cook without disturbing for 4 to 5 minutes, or until they release from the pan and are crusty and brown. Using tongs, turn the steaks over and continue to cook over high heat for another 3 to 4 minutes, or until they reach the desired doneness. Moisture will just begin to accumulate on the surface of the steaks when they are medium-rare. Remove the steaks to a plate, tent with foil to keep warm, and allow to rest for 5 minutes.

Arrange the steaks on individual plates, divide the garlic butter among the steaks, and serve immediately.

roasted garlic

Roasting garlic tames its pungent sharpness and brings out its sweet and mellow side. It's delicious added to sauces, vinaigrettes, compound butters (pages 32–33), flavored mayonnaise, mashed potatoes, hummus, or just as a simple spread for crusty bread.

To make roasted garlic, cut the stem end off a whole head of garlic to expose the cloves within. Place the garlic into a small baking dish or on a piece of foil and drizzle with extra-virgin olive oil, sprinkle with kosher salt and freshly ground black pepper, and perhaps add a few leaves of thyme or rosemary. Cover the dish with a lid or seal the foil tightly. Roast in a 350°F oven for 40 to 45 minutes, or until meltingly tender and golden brown. When the garlic is cool enough to handle, it's a breeze to peel—the cloves will pop out of their skins with a little squeeze. Since you will, no doubt, find so many delicious uses for roasted garlic, you can roast several heads at once and keep them refrigerated for up to 4 days.

tenderloin steaks
with roasted garlic sauce

This is the perfect dish for fans of roasted garlic. You can embellish the sauce by adding minced fresh herbs such as rosemary, thyme, or basil. For a more elegant presentation, blend the sauce in a blender until smooth.

Serves 4

Season the steaks generously with salt and pepper and set aside at room temperature for about 30 minutes.

Heat a large, heavy sauté pan over high heat until very hot but not smoking. Add the oil and swirl to coat the bottom of the pan. Add the steaks and cook without disturbing for 4 to 5 minutes, or until they release from the pan and are crusty and brown. Using tongs, turn the steaks over and continue to cook over high heat for another 3 to 4 minutes, or until they reach the desired doneness. Moisture will just begin to accumulate on the surface of the steaks when they are medium-rare. Remove the steaks to a plate and tent with foil to keep warm.

Reduce the heat to medium, add the wine to the pan, and simmer for a minute or so, scraping up the browned bits from the bottom of the pan with a heatproof spatula. Add the broth, cream, and garlic and simmer for another 5 to 6 minutes, or until the sauce is thickened. Stir in any accumulated juices from the steaks and season with salt and pepper to taste.

Arrange the steaks on individual plates, divide the sauce among the steaks, and serve immediately.

Four 1¼- to 1½-inch-thick beef tenderloin steaks, weighing about 8 ounces each

Kosher salt and freshly ground black pepper

2 tablespoons extra-virgin olive oil

¼ cup white wine

½ cup beef broth

½ cup heavy cream

1 head roasted garlic, cloves peeled and minced (page 30)

compound butters

Flavored, or compound, butters are a versatile alternative to sauces; like sauces, they add flavor and richness to a dish. Imagine, for instance, a perfectly seared rib-eye steak with a pat of blue cheese butter melting into it, a browned salmon fillet topped with lemon-dill butter, or rosemary–roasted garlic butter over lamb chops. Compound butters are quick and easy to prepare and can be made ahead of time. They can be flavored with garlic, fresh herbs, spices, citrus zest, and even Parmigiano-Reggiano cheese, shallots, mustard, anchovies, olives, tomatoes, or honey. They are delicious served over steaks, chops, and seafood; tossed with steamed seasonal vegetables; mixed into pasta or rice; and spread on crusty bread. The variations are endless. Compound butters keep, tightly wrapped, for several days in the refrigerator or several weeks in the freezer. Make several flavors and keep them on hand to embellish quick meals.   **Serves 8**

½ cup (1 stick) salted butter, softened
Your choice of flavoring(s), see next page

Blend the butter and flavoring(s) in a medium-size bowl.

Transfer to a sheet of plastic wrap and roll into a 1-inch-thick log. Refrigerate until firm.

To serve, cut slices of flavored butter with a warm knife. Alternatively, transfer to butter dishes to serve, or use a pastry bag to pipe rosettes. Rosettes can be piped directly onto a finished dish or onto a parchment-lined baking sheet and refrigerated until solid, at which point they will be firm enough to handle and will pop right off the parchment for serving.

For each of the variations on page 33, add the listed ingredients to the basic recipe before shaping and chilling.

lemon butter

Grated zest of 1 lemon

roasted garlic butter

3 to 4 tablespoons minced roasted garlic (page 30)

herb butter

2 to 3 tablespoons minced fresh herbs such as chives, basil, oregano, Italian parsley, thyme, dill, tarragon, rosemary, mint, or chervil

blue cheese butter

¼ to ½ cup crumbled blue cheese

port butter

For a butter with the subtle flavor of Port Reduction Sauce (page 29), try this unusual recipe. I serve it on romantic occasions. On Valentine's Day, I have even cut out pats using a small heart-shaped cookie cutter—pink "melting hearts" for my seared tenderloin steaks. Since oil and water don't mix, this recipe does require a little elbow grease or an electric mixer to blend the flavoring into the butter.

½ cup ruby port

1 shallot, minced

1 sprig fresh thyme

4 peppercorns

Combine the port, shallot, thyme, and peppercorns in a small saucepan. Bring to a boil and simmer for 7 to 8 minutes, or until very thick and syrupy.

Strain the port reduction through a fine-mesh sieve into a bowl, discard the solids, and let cool to room temperature.

tenderloin steaks with crab

This dish is fit for any special-occasion dinner and is so easy to prepare. Take the time to pick over the crabmeat for any bits of shell or cartilage. Serve with Creamed Spinach (page 139) and baked potatoes.   Serves 4

Four 1¼- to 1½-inch-thick beef tenderloin steaks, weighing about 8 ounces each

Kosher salt and freshly ground black pepper

2 tablespoons extra-virgin olive oil

2 tablespoons unsalted butter

2 cloves garlic, minced

8 ounces lump crabmeat, picked over

1 tablespoon minced Italian parsley

2 teaspoons freshly squeezed lemon juice

Season the steaks generously with salt and pepper and set aside at room temperature for about 30 minutes.

Heat a large, heavy sauté pan over high heat until very hot but not smoking. Add the oil and swirl to coat the bottom of the pan. Add the steaks and cook without disturbing for 4 to 5 minutes, or until they release from the pan and are crusty and brown. Using tongs, turn the steaks over and continue to cook over high heat for another 3 to 4 minutes, or until they reach the desired doneness. Moisture will just begin to accumulate on the surface of the steaks when they are medium-rare. Remove the steaks to a plate and tent with foil to keep warm.

Reduce the heat to low, add the butter and garlic to the pan, and sauté for 30 seconds, or until fragrant. Add the crabmeat and sauté for 2 to 3 minutes, or until heated through. Stir in the parsley and lemon juice and season with salt and pepper to taste.

Arrange the steaks on individual plates, divide the crab mixture among the steaks, and serve immediately.

beef tenderloin
with arugula

Baby arugula has a mildly peppery flavor that goes well with beef. The heat of the tenderloin slices atop the arugula causes the greens to wilt ever so slightly, creating a dish with a variety of textures and flavors. Baking tomatoes in a low oven for a long period of time takes away much of their moisture, resulting in a semidry tomato with a meaty texture and concentrated flavor. Even bland winter tomatoes become intensely flavored and delicious when treated this way. The oven-dried tomatoes add a nice sweetness to the salad and contrast well with the beef and spicy arugula. They are effortless to make, but they do take at least two hours in the oven. If you're pressed for time, substitute oil-packed sun-dried tomatoes or fresh cherry tomatoes. I serve this salad with rosemary focaccia, and, depending on what I have on hand in the refrigerator, I may toss in some black olives, diced avocados, strips of roasted red bell pepper, or grilled red onions.

Serves 4 to 6

Preheat the oven to 225°F. Toss the tomatoes with 1 tablespoon of the olive oil in a small bowl. Arrange the tomatoes skin side down on a baking sheet, season with salt and pepper, and sprinkle with the thyme. Bake for 2 to 2½ hours, or until the tomatoes are slightly dried but still tender. Let cool.

Season the tenderloin generously with salt and pepper and set aside at room temperature for about 30 minutes. Increase the oven temperature to 450°F.

Heat a large, heavy, ovenproof sauté pan over high heat until very hot but not smoking. Add the canola oil and swirl to coat the bottom of the pan. Add the tenderloin and cook without disturbing for 3 to 4 minutes, or until it releases from the pan and is crusty and brown. Using tongs, give the tenderloin a third of a turn and cook for 2 to 3 minutes more. Give the tenderloin a final third of a turn, transfer the pan to the oven, and roast the tenderloin for 24 to 28 minutes, or until it reaches the desired doneness. Moisture will just begin to accumulate on the surface of the tenderloin and a meat thermometer will

6 Roma tomatoes, cut into sixths

6 tablespoons extra-virgin olive oil

Kosher salt and freshly ground black pepper

1 teaspoon fresh thyme leaves

1 beef tenderloin roast, weighing 2½ to 3 pounds, trimmed and tied (page 41)

3 tablespoons canola oil

10 to 12 ounces baby arugula

2 tablespoons freshly squeezed lemon juice

Freshly grated Parmigiano-Reggiano cheese for serving

register 130°F when it is medium-rare. Remove the tenderloin to a plate, tent with foil to keep warm, and allow to rest for 16 to 20 minutes.

Toss the arugula and tomatoes with the remaining 5 tablespoons olive oil and the lemon juice in a large bowl and season with salt to taste. Remove the twine from the tenderloin and slice thinly against the grain.

Mound a portion of the salad in the center of each plate and sprinkle with Parmigiano-Reggiano cheese. Arrange several slices of tenderloin atop each salad and serve immediately.

pork

> "Pork cooked to medium doneness, to an internal temperature of 140°F, and rosy pink in the center is perfectly safe to eat."

Many people may not realize it, but pork that's cooked to just medium doneness, to an internal temperature of 140°F, and still rosy pink in the center is perfectly safe to eat. Today's pork is so lean that it's particularly important not to overcook it, or it will become tough and dry. Rib and loin chops, either bone-in or boneless, and pork tenderloins are best for searing. Avoid "basted" pork, which has been treated with a solution of salt, phosphate, and water, because it has a mushy, spongy texture.

- **Tenderloins:** Pork tenderloins are extremely lean and tender and have a mild flavor. Each weighs about a pound, on average, and will serve two hungry people.

- **Center-cut loin chops:** The term center-cut loin chops can refer to cuts from both the loin and the rib sections of pork. Chops from the loin are the leanest. They may be bone-in or boneless, and depending on the part of the loin that a bone-in chop comes from, it can have a piece of tenderloin attached, like a T-bone or porterhouse steak. Think of rib chops as the rib-eye of pork. They are also available bone-in or boneless. Rib chops cook up tender, juicy, and flavorful because of their higher fat content, so they are my favorite.

jerk pork tenderloin with corn and black bean salsa

In this healthful and vibrant dish, the salsa is substantial enough to be the side dish. Fresh corn kernels cut straight off the ear are best, but thawed frozen corn is a fine substitute.

Serves 4 to 6

Combine the granulated garlic, thyme, allspice, black pepper, cinnamon, nutmeg, cayenne pepper, and brown sugar in a small bowl. Season the tenderloins generously with salt and coat with the spice blend. Set aside at room temperature for about 30 minutes. Preheat the oven to 450°F.

Heat a large, heavy, ovenproof sauté pan over medium-high heat until very hot but not smoking. Add the oil and swirl to coat the bottom of the pan. Add the tenderloins and cook without disturbing for 4 to 5 minutes, or until they release from the pan and are crusty and brown. Using tongs, give the tenderloins a third of a turn and cook for 2 to 3 minutes more. Give the tenderloins a final third of a turn, transfer the pan to the oven, and roast the tenderloins for 18 to 22 minutes, or until they reach the desired doneness. Moisture will begin to pool on the surface of the tenderloins and a meat thermometer will register 140°F when they are medium. Remove the tenderloins to a plate and tent with foil to keep warm.

Set the pan over medium heat; add the onion, jalapeño, garlic, and a generous pinch of salt to the pan. Sauté for 2 to 3 minutes, or until the onion, jalapeño, and garlic are soft. Add the corn and sauté for another 2 to 3 minutes, or until the corn turns bright yellow. Add the black beans and sauté for 2 to 3 minutes more, or until the beans are heated through. Stir in the tomatoes, cilantro, cumin, lime juice, and any accumulated juices from the tenderloins and season with salt to taste.

Remove the twine from the tenderloins and slice thinly against the grain. Arrange the slices on individual plates, divide the salsa among the slices, and serve immediately.

1½ teaspoons granulated garlic

1 teaspoon ground thyme

½ teaspoon ground allspice

½ teaspoon freshly ground black pepper

¼ teaspoon ground cinnamon

¼ teaspoon freshly grated nutmeg

¼ teaspoon cayenne pepper

1½ teaspoons light brown sugar

2 pork tenderloins, weighing about 1 pound each, trimmed and tied (page 41)

Kosher salt

3 tablespoons canola oil

½ medium-size red onion, diced

1 jalapeño chile, seeded and diced

2 cloves garlic, minced

1½ cups corn kernels

One 15-ounce can black beans, rinsed and drained

2 Roma tomatoes, seeded and diced

⅓ cup minced fresh cilantro

½ teaspoon ground cumin

2 tablespoons freshly squeezed lime juice

pork tenderloin
with braised fennel sauce

This dish is rich and satisfying but healthful because the sauce is based on a vegetable puree rather than cream and butter.

Serves 4 to 6

5 tablespoons extra-virgin olive oil

2 fennel bulbs, trimmed and quartered

2 shallots, quartered

¼ cup white wine

1½ cups chicken broth

1 tablespoon crushed fennel seeds

1 tablespoon grated lemon zest

2 pork tenderloins, weighing about 1 pound each, trimmed and tied (page 41)

Kosher salt and freshly ground black pepper

Preheat the oven to 350°F. Heat a large, heavy, ovenproof sauté pan over high heat until very hot but not smoking. Add 2 tablespoons of the oil and swirl to coat the bottom of the pan. Add the fennel bulbs and shallots and cook for 8 to 10 minutes, tossing about 3 times, until crusty and brown in spots. Add the wine and simmer for a minute or so, scraping up the browned bits from the bottom of the pan with a heatproof spatula. Add the broth and bring to a boil. Cover the pan, transfer to the oven, and braise the vegetables for 40 to 45 minutes, or until tender.

Meanwhile, combine the fennel seeds and lemon zest in a small bowl. Season the tenderloins generously with salt and pepper and coat with the spice blend. Set aside at room temperature for about 30 minutes.

Carefully transfer the fennel and shallot mixture to a blender and blend until smooth. Strain the sauce through a fine-mesh sieve into a clean saucepan. Season with salt and pepper to taste and set the pan over low heat to keep warm. Increase the oven temperature to 450°F.

Heat a large, heavy sauté pan over medium-high heat until very hot but not smoking. Add the remaining 3 tablespoons oil and swirl to coat the bottom of the pan. Add the tenderloins and cook without disturbing for 4 to 5 minutes, or until they release from the pan and are crusty and brown. Using tongs, give the tenderloins a third of a turn and cook for 2 to 3 minutes more. Give the tenderloins a final third of a turn, transfer the pan to the oven, and roast the tenderloins for 18 to 22 minutes, or until they reach the desired doneness. Moisture will begin to pool on the surface of the tenderloins and a meat thermometer will register 140°F when they are medium. Remove the tenderloins to a plate, tent with foil to keep warm, and allow to rest for 10 to 12 minutes.

Remove the twine from the tenderloins and slice thinly against the grain. Arrange the slices on individual plates, divide the sauce among the slices, and serve immediately.

preparing a pork or beef tenderloin

You don't need to be a butcher to be able to prepare a whole pork or beef tenderloin for cooking. First, the silverskin, the iridescent white membrane, must be trimmed off. Although the tenderloin is the most tender cut of meat, it will be inedibly chewy if cooked with the silverskin intact. Cut away the silverskin with the tip of a very sharp boning knife. Angle the blade slightly toward the silverskin and away from the meat to minimize waste. Then, the tenderloin must be tied into a uniform shape to ensure even cooking. The tenderloin naturally tapers to one end. Obviously, this thin portion will overcook by the time the thick end is cooked properly. Fold the thin end over just far enough to create an even thickness. Tie it in place with butcher's twine. The tenderloin is now ready to cook.

tame the flame:
how to flambé

Who doesn't love the *whoosh* and flames when the alcohol is ignited in a flambéed dish? The flames can be exhilarating, or intimidating to some, but the technique is easier to master than it looks. Good ventilation is important, so have your range hood on. Do not attempt to flambé food in a nonstick pan as the high heat can ruin the coating. For safety, remove the pan from the heat before adding the liquor. Pour the liquor out of a bowl or glass into the pan, never directly from its bottle. If you are cooking over gas, ignite the alcohol by tipping the pan slightly away from you and allowing the flame to lick the contents of the pan. Use a long-handled lighter to start the flambé if you have an electric range. And don't lean over the pan as you ignite it! Once the flames start, just step back and invite your guests to watch the action. The flames will be confined to the pan and will subside within a few moments. Aside from the drama, the flambé does add an extra dimension of browned flavor to the sauce.

pork chops with brandy-mustard cream sauce

This luscious and subtle cream sauce can enhance almost any seared meat or seafood item, but it's especially nice for pork chops and beef tenderloin steaks. Serve steamed broccoli or Brussels sprouts on the side—they're delicious when slathered in the sauce.

Serves 4

Season the chops generously with salt and pepper and set aside at room temperature for about 30 minutes.

Heat a large, heavy sauté pan over medium-high heat until very hot but not smoking. Add the oil and swirl to coat the bottom of the pan. Add the chops and cook without disturbing for 4 to 5 minutes, or until they release from the pan and are crusty and brown. Using tongs, turn the chops over and continue to cook over medium-high heat for another 3 to 4 minutes, or until they reach the desired doneness. Moisture will begin to pool on the surface of the chops when they are medium. Remove the chops to a plate and tent with foil to keep warm.

Reduce the heat to medium, add the shallot to the pan, and sauté for 30 seconds, or until translucent and fragrant. Add the mustard and Worcestershire sauce. Remove the pan from the heat and carefully whisk in the brandy. Return the pan to the heat and ignite. When the flames subside, add the cream and simmer for 3 to 4 minutes, or until the sauce is thickened. Remove the pan from the heat, stir in the parsley and any accumulated juices from the chops, and season with salt and pepper to taste.

Arrange the chops on individual plates, divide the sauce among the chops, and serve immediately.

Four 1-inch-thick boneless pork loin chops, weighing about 6 ounces each

Kosher salt and freshly ground black pepper

2 tablespoons extra-virgin olive oil

1 shallot, minced

2 tablespoons Dijon mustard

1 teaspoon Worcestershire sauce

⅓ cup brandy

1 cup heavy cream

1 tablespoon minced Italian parsley

sage-rubbed pork loin chops with cranberry-pear compote

Pork chops and applesauce is a classic combination; this dish made with pears is a variation on that theme. Look for fragrant but still firm pears that will retain some texture once they're cooked. And notice that the recipe actually calls for two different types of sage—dry rubbed sage to flavor the chops and minced fresh sage for the compote. Of course, apples can be used in place of the pears.

Serves 4

Four 1-inch-thick boneless pork loin chops, weighing about 6 ounces each

Kosher salt and freshly ground black pepper

1 tablespoon dry rubbed sage

¼ cup dried cranberries

¼ cup pear or apple brandy

2 tablespoons extra-virgin olive oil

1 shallot, minced

½ cup chicken broth

1 tablespoon unsalted butter

2 firm Bartlett pears, peeled, cored, and diced

1 tablespoon minced fresh sage

Season the chops generously with salt and pepper and coat with the rubbed sage. Set aside at room temperature for about 30 minutes. Combine the cranberries and brandy in a small bowl and let soak for 16 to 20 minutes, or until the cranberries are rehydrated and pliable.

Heat a large, heavy sauté pan over medium-high heat until very hot but not smoking. Add the oil and swirl to coat the bottom of the pan. Add the chops and cook without disturbing for 4 to 5 minutes, or until they release from the pan and are crusty and brown. Using tongs, turn the chops over and continue to cook over medium-high heat for another 3 to 4 minutes, or until they reach the desired doneness. Moisture will begin to pool on the surface of the chops when they are medium. Remove the chops to a plate and tent with foil to keep warm.

Reduce the heat to medium, add the shallot to the pan, and sauté for 30 seconds, or until translucent and fragrant. Add the chicken broth, butter, pears, fresh sage, and cranberries with their soaking liquid and bring to a boil. Simmer for 6 to 7 minutes, or until the sauce is thickened. Stir in any accumulated juices from the chops and season with salt and pepper to taste.

Arrange the chops on individual plates, divide the compote among the chops, and serve immediately.

brined pork chops

Brining pork (or chicken or turkey) in a saltwater solution makes it cook up juicier and more succulent. The meat soaks up the seasoned liquid, and much of this absorbed liquid is actually retained throughout the cooking process. Brine recipes usually include sugar, maple syrup, or some other sweetener to balance the saltiness, and aromatic ingredients, such as herbs and spices, to flavor the meat through and through. The brine must be cooled to room temperature before the pork chops are added. If you are pressed for time, dissolve the salt, sugar, and flavorings in two cups of water on the stovetop as directed and then add two cups of cold water to speed the cooling time. The only disadvantage of brining is that the drippings are too salty to use for a pan sauce, so I serve these pork chops with some good Dijon mustard instead.

Serves 4

Combine the salt, brown sugar, cloves, allspice, juniper berries, bay leaves, red pepper flakes, mustard seeds, peppercorns, thyme, garlic, and water in a medium-size saucepan. Heat until the salt and sugar are dissolved. Let cool to room temperature and transfer to a large zipper-top plastic bag. Add the chops and seal the bag, letting out all the air. Brine for 24 hours in the refrigerator.

Remove the chops from the brine and set aside at room temperature for about 30 minutes. Discard the brine.

Pat the chops dry with paper towels. Heat a large, heavy sauté pan over medium-high heat until very hot but not smoking. Add the oil and swirl to coat the bottom of the pan. Add the chops and cook without disturbing for 3 to 4 minutes, or until they release from the pan and are crusty and brown. Using tongs, turn the chops over and continue to cook over medium-high heat for another 2 to 3 minutes, or until they reach the desired doneness. Moisture will begin to pool on the surface of the chops when they are medium. Remove the chops to a plate, tent with foil to keep warm, and allow to rest for 5 minutes.

Arrange the chops on individual plates and serve immediately.

2 tablespoons kosher salt

2 tablespoons light brown sugar

4 whole cloves

6 allspice berries

16 juniper berries, crushed

4 bay leaves, crumbled

½ teaspoon red pepper flakes

½ teaspoon mustard seeds

1 teaspoon black peppercorns

4 sprigs fresh thyme

10 cloves garlic, crushed

4 cups water

Four 1-inch-thick boneless pork loin chops, weighing about 6 ounces each

2 tablespoons extra-virgin olive oil

pork chops with pepper jelly glaze

My husband's amazing garden always inspires my adventures in the kitchen. A single prolific (at least by Pacific Northwest standards) serrano chile bush yielded enough fruit to make two dozen jars of spicy pepper jelly. After gifting jars to family and friends, we still had more pepper jelly than we knew what to do with. That's when this simple recipe was born. If you don't have homemade pepper jelly, it is available in any supermarket. I serve this dish with corn on the cob and coleslaw.   Serves 4

Four 1-inch-thick pork
rib chops, weighing about
10 ounces each

Kosher salt and freshly ground
black pepper

2 tablespoons canola oil

¼ cup chicken broth

¼ cup pepper jelly

Season the chops generously with salt and pepper and set aside at room temperature for about 30 minutes.

Heat a large, heavy, ovenproof sauté pan over medium-high heat until very hot but not smoking. Add the oil and swirl to coat the bottom of the pan. Add the chops and cook without disturbing for 4 to 5 minutes, or until they release from the pan and are crusty and brown. Using tongs, turn the chops over and continue to cook over medium-high heat for another 3 to 4 minutes, or until they reach the desired doneness. Moisture will begin to pool on the surface of the chops when they are medium. Remove the chops to a plate and tent with foil to keep warm.

Reduce the heat to medium, add the broth to the pan, and simmer for a minute or so, scraping up the browned bits from the bottom of the pan with a heatproof spatula. Add the jelly and stir until it melts and comes to a simmer. Stir in any accumulated juices from the chops and season with salt to taste.

Arrange the chops on individual plates, divide the glaze among the chops, and serve immediately.

lamb

"Ask your butcher to 'french' the racks, which means to expose and clean the bones, for a more elegant presentation."

Today's lamb is very tender and has a delicate, not gamy, flavor. Steaks, loin chops, rib chops, and even whole racks are good for searing. Lamb steaks and chops, like beef steaks, are best served medium-rare.

- **Lamb leg steaks:** Lamb steaks have a more robust flavor than chops, and they are slightly chewier. They are also less expensive.

- **Loin chops:** Lamb loin chops are like tiny T-bone steaks. Allow two per person.

- **Rack:** The rack comes from the rib section of the lamb and has eight ribs. It is the prime rib of lamb. The racks weigh about 1¼ pounds on average, but they can range from 1 to 1½ pounds. One rack will feed two people or four people with small appetites. Ask your butcher to "french" the racks, which means to expose and clean the bones, for a more elegant presentation.

- **Rib chops:** Lamb racks are usually cut between the ribs for lamb chops. But double-cut chops are twice as thick and include two ribs each, making for a juicier and more succulent cut that holds up to searing better. Allow two double-cut frenched chops per person or just one for those with small appetites.

lamb burgers

Even though most of us never tire of the classic beef hamburger, it's nice to mix it up once in a while. Baby lettuces and a few other simple but surprising toppings make this seared lamb patty a gourmet burger. Serve with French fries tossed with fresh rosemary and garlic.

Serves 4

Divide the ground lamb into 4 equal portions and gently form each portion into a ball. Gently pat each ball into the shape of a hamburger patty about 4½ inches across, slightly thinner in the center and thicker around the edges. Season the patties generously with salt and pepper and set aside at room temperature for about 30 minutes.

Heat a large, heavy sauté pan over medium-high heat until very hot but not smoking. Add the oil and swirl to coat the bottom of the pan. Add the patties and cook without disturbing for 4 to 5 minutes, or until they release from the pan and are crusty and brown. Using a spatula, turn the patties over and continue to cook over medium-high heat for another 3 to 4 minutes, or until they reach the desired doneness. Moisture will pool on the surface of the patties and they will be firm to the touch when they are medium-well. Remove the patties to a plate, tent with foil to keep warm, and allow to rest for 5 minutes.

Meanwhile, toast the buns, if desired. Serve the patties on the buns immediately, topped with the desired garnishes.

2 pounds ground lamb

Kosher salt and freshly ground black pepper

2 tablespoons canola oil

4 hearty hamburger buns, split

Garnishes as desired: mixed baby greens, onions, roasted red peppers, goat cheese, and/or pesto mayonnaise

lamb with tapenade

Tapenade is a paste from the south of France made with olives and other flavorings. In the summertime, try substituting fresh basil leaves for the herbes de Provence. Serve the lamb with Roasted Tomatoes (page 142) and a baguette.   Serves 4

Two 1- to 1¼-inch-thick lamb leg steaks, weighing about 1 pound each

Kosher salt and freshly ground black pepper

1 cup pitted kalamata or other brine-cured black or green olives

4½ teaspoons capers

1 anchovy fillet

1 clove garlic

1 teaspoon herbes de Provence (page 71)

1 teaspoon freshly squeezed lemon juice

5 tablespoons extra-virgin olive oil

Season the steaks generously with salt and pepper and set aside at room temperature for about 30 minutes.

Combine the olives, capers, anchovy, garlic, herbes de Provence, lemon juice, and 2 tablespoons of the oil in a food processor and pulse until smooth. Season with pepper to taste.

Heat a large, heavy sauté pan over high heat until very hot but not smoking. Add the remaining 3 tablespoons oil and swirl to coat the bottom of the pan. Add the steaks and cook without disturbing for 4 to 5 minutes, or until they release from the pan and are crusty and brown. Using tongs, turn the steaks over and continue to cook over high heat for another 2 to 3 minutes, or until they reach the desired doneness. Moisture will just begin to accumulate on the surface of the steaks when they are medium-rare. Remove the steaks to a plate, tent with foil to keep warm, and allow to rest for 8 to 10 minutes.

Slice the steaks thinly against the grain. Arrange the slices on individual plates, divide the tapenade among the slices, and serve immediately.

rosemary
lamb steaks

Garlic, rosemary, and lemon are classic flavorings for lamb. Garlic can burn and become bitter quickly when subjected to high heat, so be sure to remove it from the lamb before searing. Using sliced rather than minced garlic in the marinade makes removing the garlic much easier. Round out the meal with a Greek salad and roasted new potatoes.

Serves 4

Combine the rosemary, garlic, lemon juice, and 3 tablespoons of the oil in a large zipper-top plastic bag. Add the steaks and turn to coat. Seal the bag, letting out all the air. Marinate the steaks for at least 2 hours, or up to 24 hours, in the refrigerator.

Remove the steaks from the marinade and set aside at room temperature for about 30 minutes. Discard the marinade. Pat the steaks dry with paper towels, discard any garlic still clinging to the meat, and season generously with salt and pepper. Heat a large, heavy sauté pan over high heat until very hot but not smoking. Add the remaining 2 tablespoons oil and swirl to coat the bottom of the pan. Add the steaks and cook without disturbing for 4 to 5 minutes, or until they release from the pan and are crusty and brown. Using tongs, turn the steaks over and continue to cook over high heat for another 2 to 3 minutes, or until they reach the desired doneness. Moisture will just begin to accumulate on the surface of the steaks when they are medium-rare. Remove the steaks to a plate and tent with foil to keep warm.

Add the wine and tomato paste to the pan, and simmer for a minute or so, scraping up the browned bits from the bottom of the pan with a heatproof spatula. Add the broth and simmer for another 6 to 7 minutes, or until the sauce is thickened. Stir in any accumulated juices from the steaks and season with salt and pepper to taste.

Slice the steaks thinly against the grain. Arrange the slices on individual plates, divide the sauce among the slices, and serve immediately.

2 tablespoons minced fresh rosemary

4 cloves garlic, sliced

1 tablespoon freshly squeezed lemon juice

5 tablespoons extra-virgin olive oil

Two 1- to 1¼-inch-thick lamb leg steaks, weighing about 1 pound each

Kosher salt and freshly ground black pepper

½ cup red wine

1 tablespoon tomato paste

½ cup beef broth

lamb chops masala

Garam masala is an Indian spice blend that includes roughly equal parts of toasted and ground cardamom, cinnamon, cloves, black peppercorns, cumin, and possibly coriander or nutmeg. You can find it at most well-stocked grocery stores, or, if you are feeling more adventurous, you can make your own. Garam masala is usually added at the end of cooking so that its flavor is not lost. Serve this saucy dish with lots of Spiced Basmati Rice (page 137). Serves 4

Eight 1- to 1¼-inch-thick lamb loin chops, weighing about 5 ounces each

Kosher salt and freshly ground black pepper

2 tablespoons canola oil

1 tablespoon minced garlic

1 tablespoon minced fresh ginger

1 jalapeño chile, seeded and diced

1½ teaspoons ground cumin

One 14½-ounce can diced tomatoes, drained

½ cup heavy cream

2 tablespoons garam masala

2 tablespoons minced fresh cilantro

Season the chops generously with salt and pepper and set aside at room temperature for about 30 minutes.

Heat a large, heavy sauté pan over high heat until very hot but not smoking. Add the oil and swirl to coat the bottom of the pan. Add the chops and cook without disturbing for 4 to 5 minutes, or until they release from the pan and are crusty and brown. Using tongs, turn the chops over and continue to cook over high heat for another 2 to 3 minutes, or until they reach the desired doneness. Moisture will just begin to accumulate on the surface of the chops when they are medium-rare. Remove the chops to a plate and tent with foil to keep warm.

Reduce the heat to medium; add the garlic, ginger, and jalapeño to the pan. Sauté for 30 seconds, or until fragrant. Stir in the cumin. Add the tomatoes and cream and simmer, scraping up the browned bits from the bottom of the pan with a heatproof spatula, for 2 to 3 minutes, or until the sauce is thickened. Remove the pan from the heat; stir in the garam masala, cilantro, and any accumulated juices from the chops and season with salt to taste.

Arrange the chops on individual plates, divide the sauce among the chops, and serve immediately.

lamb chops
with balsamic syrup

Simmer some balsamic vinegar, possibly with some shallot, until it is reduced and thickened and its flavor and sweetness are concentrated, and you have balsamic syrup. Balsamic syrup is, truth be told, nothing but a substitute for very expensive, thick, aged balsamic vinegar, albeit a very delicious one. It's just sharp enough to cut through the richness of the lamb chops, and it's also great on seared duck breasts. Serve this dish with Braised Swiss Chard (page 140) and Potato Gratin (page 133) on the side. **Serves 4**

Season the chops generously with salt and pepper and set aside at room temperature for about 30 minutes.

Heat a large, heavy sauté pan over high heat until very hot but not smoking. Add the oil and swirl to coat the bottom of the pan. Add the chops and cook without disturbing for 4 to 5 minutes, or until they release from the pan and are crusty and brown. Using tongs, turn the chops over and continue to cook over high heat for another 3 to 4 minutes, or until they reach the desired doneness. Moisture will just begin to accumulate on the surface of the chops when they are medium-rare. Remove the chops to a plate and tent with foil to keep warm.

Reduce the heat to medium, add the shallot to the pan, and sauté for 30 seconds, or until translucent and fragrant. Add the vinegar and simmer, scraping up the browned bits from the bottom of the pan with a heatproof spatula, for 5 to 6 minutes, or until the sauce is thickened and slightly syrupy. Remove the pan from the heat and let cool for a minute or two. Whisk in the butter quickly, stir in any accumulated juices from the chops, and season with salt and pepper to taste.

Arrange the chops on individual plates, divide the syrup among the chops, and serve immediately.

8 double-cut frenched lamb rib chops, weighing about 5 ounces each

Kosher salt and freshly ground black pepper

3 tablespoons extra-virgin olive oil

1 shallot, minced

1 cup balsamic vinegar

2 to 3 tablespoons cold unsalted butter, diced, to your taste

lamb chops
with french lentils

French green lentils, also known as *lentilles du Puy,* retain their shape once cooked and have a firm texture and earthy flavor. Lentils require no presoaking, but they should be picked over for any stones or bits of dirt and rinsed. Save the lentil cooking liquid to use as the base for a hearty soup or stew.   Serves 4

1 cup French lentils, picked over and rinsed

½ small yellow onion

½ celery stalk

½ carrot

1 clove garlic

1 bay leaf

Kosher salt and freshly ground black pepper

8 double-cut frenched lamb rib chops, weighing about 5 ounces each

2 tablespoons red wine vinegar

2 tablespoons minced Italian parsley

1½ teaspoons Dijon mustard

1 teaspoon minced fresh thyme

½ cup extra-virgin olive oil

½ cup finely diced red onion

2 Roma tomatoes, peeled, seeded, and diced

Combine the lentils, yellow onion, celery, carrot, garlic, and bay leaf in a medium-size pot and add enough water to cover by several inches. Add several large pinches of salt. Bring to a boil and simmer for 25 to 30 minutes, or until the lentils are cooked through but still firm.

Meanwhile, season the chops generously with salt and pepper and set aside at room temperature for about 30 minutes. Whisk together the vinegar, 4½ teaspoons of the parsley, mustard, and thyme in a large bowl. Continue whisking while adding ¼ cup of the oil in a thin stream. Drain the lentils when they are tender, discarding the garlic, yellow onion, celery, carrot, and bay leaf; reserve the broth for another use. Add the lentils, red onion, and tomatoes to the vinaigrette and stir to combine. Stir in 1 more tablespoon of the oil. Season with salt and pepper to taste.

Heat a large, heavy sauté pan over high heat until very hot but not smoking. Add the remaining 3 tablespoons oil and swirl to coat the bottom of the pan. Add the chops and cook without disturbing for 4 to 5 minutes, or until they release from the pan and are crusty and brown. Using tongs, turn the chops over and continue to cook over high heat for another 3 to 4 minutes, or until they reach the desired doneness. Moisture will just begin to accumulate on the surface of the chops when they are medium-rare. Remove the chops to a plate, tent with foil to keep warm, and allow to rest for 5 minutes.

Spoon a portion of the lentil mixture into the center of each of four plates. Arrange 2 chops atop each mound of lentils and sprinkle with some of the remaining 1½ teaspoons parsley. Serve immediately.

pesto-crusted rack of lamb

Rack of lamb can be seared on the stovetop but, because of its thickness and the shape of its bones, must be finished with the indirect heat of the oven. In this recipe, the basil pesto is slathered onto the lamb after it is seared so that it does not burn. Roasted Tomatoes (page 142) are the perfect side dish.

Serves 4

Season the lamb generously with salt and pepper and set aside at room temperature for about 30 minutes. Combine the basil, garlic, pine nuts, Parmigiano-Reggiano cheese, and 2 tablespoons of the oil in a food processor and pulse until smooth. Preheat the oven to 400°F.

Heat a large, heavy, ovenproof sauté pan over high heat until very hot but not smoking. Add the remaining 2 tablespoons oil and swirl to coat the bottom of the pan. Add the lamb, fat side down, and cook without disturbing for 4 to 5 minutes, or until it releases from the pan and is crusty and brown. Using tongs, turn the lamb over, and with a spoon, spread the pesto evenly over the top and sides. Transfer the pan to the oven and roast the racks for 16 to 20 minutes, or until they reach the desired doneness. Moisture will just begin to accumulate on the surface of the lamb and a meat thermometer will register 130°F when it is medium-rare. Remove the lamb to a plate, tent with foil to keep warm, and allow to rest for 10 to 15 minutes.

Carve the lamb racks into chops by slicing between the ribs. Arrange the chops on individual plates and serve immediately.

---

2 frenched lamb racks, weighing about 1¼ pounds each

Kosher salt and freshly ground black pepper

1½ cups fresh basil

2 cloves garlic, minced

2 tablespoons pine nuts

2 tablespoons freshly grated Parmigiano-Reggiano cheese

¼ cup extra-virgin olive oil

chicken, duck, and quail

"Start the chicken on the stovetop to achieve a crispy brown crust, and finish it in the oven until it's cooked through."

chicken

When it comes to searing chicken, boneless, skin-on chicken breasts are best. The skin cooks up irresistibly crunchy and protects the lean flesh, helping it to stay juicy. Bone-in breasts are good too, but they will not brown as well on the bone side, and they make for a less elegant presentation.

The direct heat of stovetop searing browns the surface of an item, leaving the center medium-rare. That's great for steaks and chops, but it means that chicken seared on the stove would still be raw in the center. And if the chicken were seared long enough to cook all the way through, the skin would burn. The solution to this problem is to use indirect heat in combination with direct heat. Simply put, start the chicken on the stovetop to achieve a crispy brown crust, and finish it in the oven until it's cooked through. Remember to use a pan with an ovenproof handle.

Chicken must be cooked to an internal temperature of 165°F to be safe to eat. For perfectly cooked, tender, and juicy chicken, remove it from the oven when a meat thermometer registers 160°F. The residual heat and the resulting carryover cooking will allow the chicken to reach 165°F as it rests, tented with foil.

duck

You've probably noticed by now that the technique for searing is basically the same no matter what you're cooking. But duck breasts are the exception to the rule—they are cooked over lower heat and do not require oil. This is because the skin of the duck breast has a thick layer of fat (the flesh, however, is very lean). The duck breast actually cooks in its own rendered fat, and the skin becomes delectably golden brown and crunchy, like cracklings.

It takes time for the fat to render—just think of cooking bacon. Scoring the skin of the duck breasts helps the process along. Start the breasts over medium heat, and adjust the heat as necessary. If the breasts brown after just a few moments in the pan and the fat hasn't had time to cook out, turn down the heat. On the other hand, if the duck breasts are still soft and pale after several minutes, crank up the heat. Since fat acts as an insulator, the duck will cook for a relatively long time on the skin side and still remain rosy in the center. Duck is considered a red meat and the breasts are best enjoyed medium-rare. By the way, don't throw out the rendered duck fat—strain it, store it in the refrigerator or freezer, and use it for making the best fried potatoes imaginable.

If you have trouble finding duck breasts at your local butcher, try www.nickyusa.com. I recommend their Muscovy hen breasts.

a must-have tool:
the digital probe thermometer

I swear by my digital probe thermometer and highly recommend investing in one. This inexpensive tool allows you to monitor the internal temperature of meat throughout the cooking process. You simply set your target temperature, insert the probe into the center of the thickest part of the meat, put the pan in the oven, and place the display on the counter beside the oven. The oven door closes right over the probe wire. An alarm will sound when the meat's internal temperature reaches the target temperature. A digital probe thermometer is great for cooking beef and pork tenderloin, rack of lamb, chicken breasts, or roasts of any kind, and it can even be used as a candy/jelly/deep-fry thermometer. It's one handy little gadget that will make you look like a cooking genius—it takes the guesswork out of determining when the meat is done and ensures perfect results every single time. Digital probe thermometers are available at most cookware shops for about $30.

chicken breasts with mushroom, paprika, and sour cream gravy

Paprika is not just for color! Its sweet and earthy flavor really comes through in this Hungarian-inspired dish. Serve the chicken with spaetzle, pasta, rice, mashed potatoes, or anything else that will sop up the tasty sauce.

Serves 4

Season the chicken breasts generously with salt and pepper and set aside at room temperature for about 30 minutes. Preheat the oven to 375°F.

Heat a large, heavy, ovenproof sauté pan over high heat until very hot but not smoking. Add the oil and swirl to coat the bottom of the pan. Add the chicken breasts, skin side down, and cook without disturbing for 4 to 5 minutes, or until they release from the pan and are crusty and brown. Using tongs, turn the chicken breasts over, transfer the pan to the oven, and roast the chicken for 16 to 20 minutes, or until it is just cooked through. The chicken breasts will be firm to the touch, the juices will run clear, and a meat thermometer will register 160°F. Remove the chicken breasts to a plate and tent with foil; the internal temperature should rise to 165°F.

Set the pan over medium heat; add the onion, mushrooms, and a generous pinch of salt; and sauté for 4 to 5 minutes, or until the vegetables are soft. Add the flour and paprika and stir until well incorporated. Add the wine and broth. Bring to a boil, stirring constantly and scraping up the browned bits from the bottom of the pan with a heatproof spatula, and simmer for 2 to 3 minutes, or until the sauce is thickened. Remove the pan from the heat, stir in the sour cream and any accumulated juices from the chicken, and season with salt and pepper to taste.

Arrange the chicken breasts on individual plates, divide the sauce among the chicken breasts, and serve immediately.

4 boneless, skin-on chicken breasts

Kosher salt and freshly ground black pepper

3 tablespoons canola oil

½ medium-size yellow onion, diced

8 ounces button mushrooms, sliced

2 tablespoons all-purpose flour

3 tablespoons Hungarian paprika

2 tablespoons white wine

1½ cups chicken broth

⅓ cup sour cream

smoky chicken breasts with sherry sauce

Spanish smoked paprika, also known as *pimentón*, has a unique and complex flavor, at once smoky, spicy, sweet, and earthy. It can be used as a spice rub all by itself and transforms a plain chicken breast into a delectable dish. This spice is available in both sweet and hot varieties. I prefer the sweet version, since the heat doesn't overwhelm the flavor when it's used in quantity. Most gourmet markets stock Spanish paprika.   Serves 4

2 tablespoons sweet Spanish paprika

¼ cup extra-virgin olive oil

4 boneless, skin-on chicken breasts

Kosher salt and freshly ground black pepper

1 shallot, minced

¼ cup sherry

¾ cup chicken broth

1 teaspoon sherry vinegar

2 to 3 tablespoons cold unsalted butter, diced, to your taste

Combine the paprika and 2 tablespoons of the oil in a large zipper-top plastic bag. Add the chicken breasts and turn to coat. Seal the bag, letting out all the air. Marinate the chicken breasts for at least 2 hours, or up to 24 hours, in the refrigerator.

Remove the chicken breasts from the marinade, season generously with salt and pepper, and set aside at room temperature for about 30 minutes. Discard the marinade. Preheat the oven to 375°F.

Heat a large, heavy, ovenproof sauté pan over high heat until very hot but not smoking. Add the remaining 2 tablespoons oil and swirl to coat the bottom of the pan. Add the chicken breasts, skin side down, and cook without disturbing for 4 to 5 minutes, or until they release from the pan and are crusty and brown. Using tongs, turn the chicken breasts over, transfer the pan to the oven, and roast the chicken for 16 to 20 minutes, or until it is just cooked through. The chicken breasts will be firm to the touch, the juices will run clear, and a meat thermometer will register 160°F. Remove the chicken breasts to a plate and tent with foil; the internal temperature should rise to 165°F.

Set the pan over medium heat, add the shallot to the pan, and sauté for 30 seconds, or until translucent and fragrant. Add the sherry and simmer for a minute or so, scraping up the browned bits from the bottom of the pan with a heatproof spatula. Add the broth and simmer for another 6 to 7 minutes, or until the sauce is thickened. Remove the pan from the heat and let cool for a minute or two. Whisk in the vinegar and butter quickly, stir in any accumulated juices from the chicken breasts, and season with salt and pepper to taste.

Arrange the chicken breasts on individual plates, divide the sauce among the chicken breasts, and serve immediately.

firecracker chicken breasts with mango sauce

With a zippy spice rub and a spicy, sweet, and sour sauce, this chicken is hot! Despite the long list of ingredients, the recipe is simple and straightforward to prepare. Be sure to wear gloves when handling the habanero and use caution when pureeing the steaming-hot sauce. Serve the chicken with couscous or Spiced Basmati Rice (page 137).   **Serves 4**

2 teaspoons pure chile powder (page 22)

2 teaspoons ground cumin

1 teaspoon ground coriander

½ teaspoon ground cinnamon

½ teaspoon cayenne pepper

½ teaspoon freshly ground black pepper

¼ cup canola oil

4 boneless, skin-on chicken breasts

Kosher salt

¼ cup diced yellow onion

2 cloves garlic, minced

1 habanero chile, seeded and diced

1 large ripe mango, peeled and diced

3 tablespoons freshly squeezed lime juice

2 tablespoons light brown sugar

¾ cup water

Combine the chile powder, cumin, coriander, cinnamon, cayenne pepper, black pepper, and 2 tablespoons of the oil in a large zipper-top plastic bag. Add the chicken breasts and turn to coat. Seal the bag, letting out all the air. Marinate the chicken breasts for at least 2 hours, or up to 24 hours, in the refrigerator.

Remove the chicken breasts from the marinade, season generously with salt, and set aside at room temperature for about 30 minutes. Discard the marinade. Preheat the oven to 375°F.

Heat a large, heavy, ovenproof sauté pan over high heat until very hot but not smoking. Add the remaining 2 tablespoons oil and swirl to coat the bottom of the pan. Add the chicken breasts, skin side down, and cook without disturbing for 4 to 5 minutes, or until they release from the pan and are crusty and brown. Using tongs, turn the chicken breasts over, transfer the pan to the oven, and roast the chicken for 16 to 20 minutes, or until it is just cooked through. The chicken breasts will be firm to the touch, the juices will run clear, and a meat thermometer will register 160°F. Remove the chicken breasts to a plate and tent with foil; the internal temperature should rise to 165°F.

Set the pan over medium heat; add the onion, garlic, and habanero; and sauté for 2 to 3 minutes, or until soft. Add the mango, lime juice, and brown sugar and simmer, scraping up the browned bits from the bottom of the pan with a heatproof spatula, for 3 to 4 minutes, or until the mango is soft. Transfer the sauce to a blender, add the water, and blend until smooth. Season with salt to taste.

Arrange the chicken breasts on individual plates, divide the sauce among the chicken breasts, and serve immediately.

five-spice-rubbed duck breasts with red currant glaze

Duck breasts and fruity sauce is a classic combination, but the five-spice powder adds an exotic twist.

Serves 4

4 boneless, skin-on duck breasts, weighing about 8 ounces each

Kosher salt

2 teaspoons five-spice powder

Juice of 1 orange

½ teaspoon grated orange zest

1 cup red currant jelly

Freshly ground black pepper

With a knife, score the skin of each duck breast in a diamond pattern, being careful not to pierce the flesh. Season the duck generously with salt and rub with the five-spice powder. Set aside at room temperature for about 30 minutes.

Heat a large, heavy sauté pan over medium heat until very hot but not smoking. Add the duck breasts, skin side down, and cook without disturbing for 7 to 8 minutes, or until the skin is dark brown and crispy and the fat has rendered. Using tongs, turn the duck breasts over and continue to cook over medium heat for another 3 to 4 minutes, or until they reach the desired doneness. The duck will just begin to feel firm to the touch when it is medium-rare. Remove the duck to a plate and tent with foil to keep warm. Pour off all of the accumulated fat from the pan and reserve for another use.

Add the orange juice to the pan and simmer for a minute or so, scraping up the browned bits from the bottom of the pan with a heatproof spatula. Add the orange zest and jelly and stir until the jelly melts and comes to a simmer. Stir in any accumulated juices from the duck and season with salt and pepper to taste.

Slice the duck breasts thinly against the grain. Arrange the slices on individual plates, divide the glaze among the slices, and serve immediately.

duck breasts
with blood orange sauce

Bright and bold, this dish is a contemporary take on the classic duck à l'orange and requires just four ingredients. The brilliant, jewel-colored blood orange syrup has a delicate floral flavor and is at once sweet, tart, and bitter, cutting right through the richness of the duck. Blood oranges have a short winter season. Serve these duck breasts with Quinoa Pilaf (page 136). If you like, add a final flourish by garnishing them with blood orange suprêmes (page 99) or long strips of zest. Serves 4

With a knife, score the skin of each duck breast in a diamond pattern, being careful not to pierce the flesh. Season the duck generously with salt and pepper. Set aside at room temperature for about 30 minutes.

Heat a large, heavy sauté pan over medium heat until very hot but not smoking. Add the duck breasts, skin side down, and cook without disturbing for 7 to 8 minutes, or until the skin is dark brown and crispy and the fat has rendered. Using tongs, turn the duck breasts over and continue to cook over medium heat for another 3 to 4 minutes, or until they reach the desired doneness. The duck will just begin to feel firm to the touch when it is medium-rare. Remove the duck to a plate and tent with foil to keep warm. Pour off all of the accumulated fat from the pan and reserve for another use.

Add the orange juice to the pan and simmer, scraping up the browned bits from the bottom of the pan with a heatproof spatula, for 5 to 6 minutes, or until the sauce is thickened and slightly syrupy. Stir in any accumulated juices from the duck and season with salt and pepper to taste.

Slice the duck breasts thinly against the grain. Arrange the slices on individual plates, divide the sauce among the slices, and serve immediately.

4 boneless, skin-on duck breasts, weighing about 8 ounces each

Kosher salt and freshly ground black pepper

Juice of 6 blood oranges, strained through a fine-mesh sieve

duck breasts
with blackberry-port sauce

Blackberries bring out the fruity character of ruby port. And, since duck has a natural affinity for sweet and tart fruit, the flavors of this dish simply belong together. Frozen berries can be used in place of fresh ones, but for the best results, the berries must maintain their plump shape once defrosted. To thaw the berries, arrange them in a single layer on a paper towel–lined plate and leave them at room temperature for about an hour. Try Braised Swiss Chard (page 140) on the side.   Serves 4

4 boneless, skin-on
duck breasts, weighing
about 8 ounces each

Kosher salt and freshly ground
black pepper

1 shallot, diced

1 cup ruby port

1 sprig fresh thyme

¼ cup seedless blackberry
preserves

1 cup fresh blackberries

With a knife, score the skin of each duck breast in a diamond pattern, being careful not to pierce the flesh. Season the duck generously with salt and pepper. Set aside at room temperature for about 30 minutes.

Heat a large, heavy sauté pan over medium heat until very hot but not smoking. Add the duck breasts, skin side down, and cook without disturbing for 7 to 8 minutes, or until the skin is dark brown and crispy and the fat has rendered. Using tongs, turn the duck breasts over and continue to cook over medium heat for another 3 to 4 minutes, or until they reach the desired doneness. The duck will just begin to feel firm to the touch when it is medium-rare. Remove the duck to a plate and tent with foil to keep warm. Pour off all of the accumulated fat from the pan and reserve for another use.

Add the shallot to the pan and sauté for 30 seconds, or until translucent and fragrant. Add the port, thyme, and preserves and simmer, scraping up the browned bits from the bottom of the pan with a heatproof spatula, for 6 to 7 minutes, or until the sauce is thickened and slightly syrupy. Discard the thyme. Add the berries and simmer for another minute or so. Stir in any accumulated juices from the duck and season with salt and pepper to taste.

Slice the duck breasts thinly against the grain. Arrange the slices on individual plates, divide the sauce among the slices, and serve immediately.

duck with vanilla bean jus

Vanilla isn't just for ice cream anymore! This may come as a surprise, but vanilla's bold flavor can enhance savory as well as sweet foods. The deep flavor of the whole beans and the visual appeal of their tiny seeds are the keys to this sauce, so don't substitute vanilla extract. Look for fresh vanilla beans, which should be fragrant and pliable, at gourmet markets and specialty stores. Serve Potato Gratin (page 133) or Baked Sweet Potatoes (page 135) on the side.

Serves 4

With a knife, score the skin of each duck breast in a diamond pattern, being careful not to pierce the flesh. Season the duck generously with salt and pepper. Set aside at room temperature for about 30 minutes.

Heat a large, heavy sauté pan over medium heat until very hot but not smoking. Add the duck breasts, skin side down, and cook without disturbing for 7 to 8 minutes, or until the skin is dark brown and crispy and the fat has rendered. Using tongs, turn the duck breasts over and continue to cook over medium heat for another 3 to 4 minutes, or until they reach the desired doneness. The duck will just begin to feel firm to the touch when it is medium-rare. Remove the duck to a plate and tent with foil to keep warm. Pour off all of the accumulated fat from the pan and reserve for another use.

Add the shallot to the pan and sauté for 30 seconds, or until translucent and fragrant. Add the wine and simmer for a minute or so, scraping up the browned bits from the bottom of the pan with a heatproof spatula. With a paring knife, cut the vanilla bean in half lengthwise. With the tip of the knife, scrape out the seeds and add both the seeds and the pod to the pan. Add the broth and brandy and simmer for another 6 to 7 minutes, or until the sauce is thickened. Stir in any accumulated juices from the duck and season with salt and pepper to taste.

Slice the duck breasts thinly against the grain. Arrange the slices on individual plates, divide the jus among the slices, and garnish with pieces of the vanilla bean. Serve immediately.

4 boneless, skin-on duck breasts, weighing about 8 ounces each

Kosher salt and freshly ground black pepper

1 shallot, minced

¼ cup red wine

1 vanilla bean

1 cup chicken or duck broth

1 tablespoon brandy

provençal
duck breasts

The vibrant flavors of southern France inspired this recipe. In sunny Provence, lavender honey is prized for its delicate floral character, and green peppercorns are used whenever a milder pepper flavor is desired. The honey in the marinade will cause the duck breasts to brown much more quickly than usual. Watch them carefully and turn the heat down if they darken too quickly. Lavender honey, green peppercorns, and herbes de Provence can be found at most gourmet markets as well as many supermarkets.

Serves 4

4 boneless, skin-on duck breasts, weighing about 8 ounces each

3 tablespoons lavender honey

1 teaspoon herbes de Provence (page 71)

Kosher salt

1 teaspoon freshly cracked green peppercorns

1 shallot, minced

½ cup red wine

½ cup chicken or duck broth

Freshly ground black pepper

With a knife, score the skin of each duck breast in a diamond pattern, being careful not to pierce the flesh. Combine the honey and herbes de Provence in a large zipper-top plastic bag. Add the duck and turn to coat. Seal the bag, letting out all the air. Marinate the duck for at least 2 hours, or up to 24 hours, in the refrigerator.

Remove the duck from the marinade and set aside at room temperature for about 30 minutes. Discard the marinade.

Pat the duck dry with paper towels, season generously with salt, and sprinkle with the green peppercorns. Heat a large, heavy sauté pan over medium heat until very hot but not smoking. Add the duck breasts, skin side down, and cook without disturbing for 7 to 8 minutes, or until the skin is dark brown and crispy and the fat has rendered. Using tongs, turn the duck breasts over and continue to cook over medium heat for another 3 to 4 minutes, or until they reach the desired doneness. The duck will just begin to feel firm to the touch when it is medium-rare. Remove the duck to a plate and tent with foil to keep warm. Pour off all of the accumulated fat from the pan and reserve for another use.

Add the shallot to the pan and sauté for 30 seconds, or until translucent and fragrant. Add the wine and simmer for a minute or so, scraping up the browned bits from the bottom of the pan with a heatproof spatula. Add the broth and simmer for another 8 to 10 minutes, or until the sauce is thickened. Stir in any accumulated juices from the duck and season with salt and pepper to taste.

Slice the duck breasts thinly against the grain. Arrange the slices on individual plates, divide the sauce among the slices, and serve immediately.

herbes de provence

In the south of France the ubiquitous seasoning blend herbes de Provence is sprinkled on everything from rotisserie chicken to pizza. The aromatic mélange typically includes rosemary, thyme, basil, marjoram, savory, and lavender. Fortunately, you don't have to mix your own herbs; the blend can be found prepackaged in gourmet shops and supermarkets. Read the list of ingredients to make sure they look authentic; many so-called herbes de Provence sold in this country do not resemble the blends from France at all and include dried orange or lemon zest and garlic or onion. I usually make my own spice and herb blends, but this is the only one I always buy.

foie gras and cherry salad

Foie gras, the liver of fattened goose or duck, has a soft, silky texture and rich flavor. Pan-searing best brings out these qualities and is a quick and easy way to prepare this luxurious ingredient. Since foie gras is mostly fat, there is no need to add oil to the pan. Be very careful to sear it quickly over very high heat; otherwise, the liver will melt away before your eyes. The fat rendered once the foie gras is cooked becomes a part of the warm Sauternes vinaigrette. Tender leaves of butter lettuce cup the foie gras, cherries, and dressing. Serve this as a first course at an elegant dinner party.   Serves 4

¼ cup dried pitted tart cherries, such as Montmorency

½ cup Sauternes

Four 1-inch-thick slices foie gras, weighing 3 to 4 ounces each

Kosher salt and freshly ground black pepper

1 shallot, minced

3 to 4 tablespoons cider vinegar, to your taste

1 head butter lettuce, leaves separated

Combine the cherries and Sauternes in a small bowl and let soak for 10 to 12 minutes, or until the cherries are rehydrated and tender.

Season the foie gras generously with salt and pepper. Heat a large, heavy sauté pan over high heat until very hot but not smoking. Add the foie gras and cook without disturbing for 1 to 2 minutes, or until it releases from the pan and is crusty and brown. Using tongs, turn the foie gras over and continue to cook over high heat for another minute, or until it reaches the desired doneness. The foie gras will be soft to the touch when it is medium-rare. Remove the foie gras to a plate and tent with foil to keep warm.

Reduce the heat to medium, add the shallot to the pan, and sauté for 30 seconds, or until translucent and fragrant. Add the cherry mixture and vinegar and simmer, scraping up the browned bits from the bottom of the pan with a heatproof spatula, for 3 to 4 minutes, or until the sauce is thickened and slightly syrupy. Season with salt and pepper to taste.

Arrange several lettuce leaves in the center of each of four plates. Arrange a slice of foie gras atop each salad and drizzle with the vinaigrette. Serve immediately.

buffalo quail with southwestern ranch dressing

My love of spicy, crunchy buffalo wings inspired me to create this dish, with quail being more succulent and meaty, and certainly more sophisticated, than chicken. Quail has dark meat and is best served medium-rare. The birds are tiny, weighing only about four ounces each, so allow two quail per person for a main course. Semiboneless quail have had all of their bones removed except for the wing and leg bones, making them easier to cook and eat. Look for them at your local butcher shop or order them from www.nickyusa.com.

Serves 4

Season the quail generously with salt and pepper and set aside at room temperature for about 30 minutes. Combine the sour cream, buttermilk, cilantro, chiles, garlic, and cumin in a food processor and pulse until smooth. Season with salt and pepper to taste. Combine the melted butter and hot sauce in a large bowl.

Heat a very large, heavy sauté pan over high heat until very hot but not smoking. Add the oil and swirl to coat the bottom of the pan. Add the quail, breast side down, and cook without disturbing for 2 to 3 minutes, or until they release from the pan and are crusty and brown. Using tongs, turn the quail over and continue to cook over high heat for another 2 to 3 minutes, or until they reach the desired doneness. The quail will just begin to feel firm to the touch when they are medium-rare. Remove the quail to a plate and tent with foil to keep warm. Toss the quail with the hot sauce, two at a time.

Mound a portion of greens in the center of each plate. Arrange 2 quail atop each salad and drizzle with the dressing. Serve immediately.

8 semiboneless quail

Kosher salt and freshly ground black pepper

¾ cup sour cream

½ cup buttermilk

½ cup minced fresh cilantro

2 serrano chiles, seeded and diced

1 clove garlic, minced

Generous pinch of ground cumin

¼ cup (½ stick) unsalted butter, melted

¼ cup hot sauce, such as Tabasco

3 tablespoons canola oil

8 ounces mesclun greens

seafood

"Shrimp curl head to tail as they are subjected to heat: They will tell you C for 'cooked' and O for 'overcooked.'"

shellfish

Shrimp are a great choice for quick meals because they cook in a matter of moments. They are sold by size; the smaller the number, the larger the shrimp. For example, 16/20 count means there are between 16 and 20 shrimp in a pound. Opt for wild American shrimp, which have a sweet flavor, rather than imported and farm-raised, which can taste muddy. And to cut down on preparation time, choose shrimp that have already been peeled and deveined.

Perfectly cooked shrimp are tender and moist. There are several ways to tell when shrimp are cooked through. First, the texture will firm up. Second, the flesh will change from translucent to opaque, and no matter what the variety or color when raw, all shrimp turn pink and white when cooked. Finally, shrimp curl head to tail as they are subjected to heat. Look closely as they cook, and they will tell you C for "cooked" and O for "overcooked"!

When shopping for sea scallops, select only those labeled "dry" from a reputable fishmonger. "Wet" scallops, which are soaked in a phosphate solution to increase their weight and help preserve them, will exude liquid as soon as they hit the heat—they will simmer in their own juices and never brown. When preparing scallops, take the time to remove the white, crescent-shaped bit of tissue known as the foot, which when cooked has the texture of rubber bands.

Sea scallops are at their juiciest and most tender when they are cooked to medium-rare or medium. When they are brown on the surface but still feel slightly soft to the touch, they are done. Another sure sign that they are ready is when moisture begins to accumulate on the surface of the scallops. The center of the scallops will remain slightly translucent.

fish

Any firm-textured or meaty fish is good for searing. Salmon, tuna, halibut, mahi-mahi, and swordfish are all good choices. Select fresh fish over previously frozen fish, which exudes so much water as it cooks that it does not brown well. Both steaks and thick fillets work well, but boneless, skinless fillets make for the most elegant presentation and pleasant eating.

Fish fillets will not stick to a properly preheated pan, but their relatively delicate texture can make them a bit more difficult to flip than beef, pork, lamb, or even shrimp or scallops. If you're hesitant about using a regular sauté pan, a large, heavy nonstick pan is acceptable for searing fish. The fish may not become quite as brown and crispy as in a regular pan, but it will slide right out. Add the cooking oil to the nonstick pan before preheating it—this prevents the pan from overheating—and continue with the recipe as directed. Using a very thin, wide, and flexible spatula, such as a fish spatula, also makes turning fish easier.

Fish should be seared until it is just cooked through but still moist. To tell if a piece of fish is done, press it gently with one finger. It is ready if it just begins to flake. (Some say that the fish should flake easily when cooked, but I find that it has dried out by the time it reaches that point.) Some fish, such as tuna and salmon, are best served rare or medium-rare and will feel soft and slightly gelatinous when ready. You can also check if fish is cooked through by piercing the center of the fish with the tip of a paring knife, holding it there for about 15 seconds, and then carefully bringing the tip of the knife to your lip, which is very sensitive. When the knife feels slightly hot to the touch, the fish is done. Use both of these tests together, and you will have perfectly cooked fish every time.

shrimp with warm tomato vinaigrette

This shrimp dish becomes a complete meal when served on a bed of salad greens and with toasted baguette slices to soak up the vinaigrette.

Serves 4

1 pound extra-large shrimp (16/20 count), peeled and deveined

Kosher salt and freshly ground black pepper

¼ cup plus 2 tablespoons extra-virgin olive oil

1 shallot, minced

1 tablespoon tomato paste

2 Roma tomatoes, peeled, seeded, and diced

1 teaspoon Dijon mustard

2 tablespoons red wine vinegar

1 tablespoon minced Italian parsley

Season the shrimp generously with salt and pepper and set aside at room temperature for about 30 minutes.

Heat a large, heavy sauté pan over high heat until very hot but not smoking. Add 2 tablespoons of the oil and swirl to coat the bottom of the pan. Add the shrimp and cook without disturbing for 1 to 2 minutes, or until they release from the pan and are crusty and brown. Using tongs, turn the shrimp over and continue to cook over high heat for another 1 to 2 minutes, or until they are just cooked through. The shrimp will be firm to the touch, the color will be opaque and pink, and they will begin to curl. Remove the shrimp to a plate and tent with foil to keep warm.

Reduce the heat to medium, add the shallot to the pan, and sauté for 30 seconds, or until translucent and fragrant. Stir in the tomato paste. Add the tomatoes and sauté for another 1 to 2 minutes, or until soft. Remove the pan from the heat and let cool for a minute or two. Stir in the mustard, vinegar, parsley, and any accumulated juices from the shrimp. Whisk in the remaining ¼ cup oil and season with salt and pepper to taste.

Arrange the shrimp on individual plates, divide the vinaigrette among the shrimp, and serve immediately.

garlic shrimp
with spanish chorizo

This dish was inspired by the classic Spanish tapa *gambas al ajillo,* shrimp seared in garlic oil. The addition of Spanish chorizo makes this a more substantial version, enough for either a hearty appetizer or a light main course when accompanied by a green salad and plenty of crusty bread. Do not confuse Mexican chorizo with Spanish chorizo—the Spanish variety, which is available at most gourmet delis, is cured and ready to eat, whereas the Mexican kind is a fresh sausage and must be cooked.   **Serves 4**

Season the shrimp generously with salt and pepper and set aside at room temperature for about 30 minutes.

Heat a large, heavy sauté pan over high heat until very hot but not smoking. Add 2 tablespoons of the oil and swirl to coat the bottom of the pan. Add the shrimp and cook without disturbing for 1 to 2 minutes, or until they release from the pan and are crusty and brown. Using tongs, turn the shrimp over, add the chorizo, and continue to cook over high heat for another 1 to 2 minutes, or until the shrimp are just cooked through. The shrimp will be firm to the touch, the color will be opaque and pink, and they will begin to curl. Reduce the heat to medium-low and add the remaining 2 tablespoons oil. Add the garlic and red pepper flakes and stir for a minute or so until fragrant. Season with salt and pepper to taste.

Arrange the shrimp and chorizo mixture on individual plates and serve immediately.

1 pound extra-large shrimp (16/20 count), peeled and deveined

Kosher salt and freshly ground black pepper

¼ cup extra-virgin olive oil

4 ounces Spanish chorizo, thinly sliced

1 tablespoon minced garlic

Generous pinch of red pepper flakes, or to taste

shrimp with red pepper rémoulade

Serve this dish as an appetizer, or—to create a more substantial meal—pile the shrimp and rémoulade, along with some shredded lettuce and sliced tomato, inside a split baguette, like a po' boy sandwich.

Serves 4

1 pound extra-large shrimp (16/20 count), peeled and deveined

Kosher salt and freshly ground black pepper

½ cup mayonnaise

½ cup diced roasted red bell pepper (page 92)

¼ cup sliced green onions

¼ cup Italian parsley

1 anchovy fillet

1 clove garlic

1 tablespoon freshly squeezed lemon juice

1 tablespoon tomato paste

1 tablespoon capers

2 teaspoons pure chile powder (page 22)

1 teaspoon Dijon mustard

½ teaspoon Worcestershire sauce

Several drops of hot sauce, such as Tabasco, to your taste

2 tablespoons extra-virgin olive oil

Season the shrimp generously with salt and pepper and set aside at room temperature for about 30 minutes.

Combine the mayonnaise, bell pepper, green onions, parsley, anchovy, garlic, lemon juice, tomato paste, capers, chile powder, mustard, Worcestershire sauce, and hot sauce in a food processor and pulse until smooth. Season with salt and pepper to taste.

Heat a large, heavy sauté pan over high heat until very hot but not smoking. Add the oil and swirl to coat the bottom of the pan. Add the shrimp and cook without disturbing for 1 to 2 minutes, or until they release from the pan and are crusty and brown. Using tongs, turn the shrimp over and continue to cook over high heat for another 1 to 2 minutes, or until they are just cooked through. The shrimp will be firm to the touch, the color will be opaque and pink, and they will begin to curl.

Arrange the shrimp on individual plates, divide the rémoulade among the shrimp, and serve immediately.

coconut-curry scallops

Canned coconut milk is what makes this dish, yielding a luscious, flavorful sauce with a silky texture. In the can the coconut cream always rises to the top, so to recombine, shake the can well before opening. (Be sure to buy coconut milk and not cream of coconut.) Serve the scallops with Spiced Basmati Rice (page 137) and accompany the dish with a salad of cucumber, pineapple, red onion, cilantro, and lime juice.

Serves 4

Gently pat the scallops dry with paper towels. Season them generously with salt and pepper and set aside at room temperature for about 30 minutes.

Heat a large, heavy sauté pan over high heat until very hot but not smoking. Add the oil and swirl to coat the bottom of the pan. Add the scallops and cook without disturbing for 2 to 3 minutes, or until they release from the pan and are crusty and brown. Using tongs, turn the scallops over and continue to cook over high heat for another 1 to 2 minutes, or until they reach the desired doneness. Moisture will just begin to accumulate on the surface of the scallops when they are medium-rare. Remove the scallops to a plate and tent with foil to keep warm.

Reduce the heat to medium; add the garlic, ginger, and jalapeño to the pan; and sauté for 30 seconds, or until fragrant. Stir in the curry powder. Add the coconut milk and simmer, scraping up the browned bits from the bottom of the pan with a heatproof spatula, for 5 to 6 minutes, or until the sauce is thickened. Remove the pan from the heat; stir in the cilantro, lime juice, and any accumulated juices from the scallops, and season with salt to taste.

Arrange the scallops on individual plates, divide the sauce among the scallops, and serve immediately.

12 large sea scallops (about 1 pound), feet removed

Kosher salt and freshly ground black pepper

3 tablespoons canola oil

1 tablespoon minced garlic

1 tablespoon minced fresh ginger

1 jalapeño chile, seeded and diced

1 tablespoon curry powder

One 14-ounce can coconut milk

2 tablespoons minced fresh cilantro

2 teaspoons freshly squeezed lime juice

scallops with mushroom cream sauce

This dish is my interpretation of the French classic *coquilles St. Jacques*, in which the scallops are simmered with mushrooms in a cream sauce, replaced in their shells, and finished under the broiler. I prefer to sear the scallops to add another layer of flavor and texture to the dish. These scallops make a rich appetizer or a light main course.

Serves 4

¼ cup panko bread crumbs

1 tablespoon unsalted butter, melted

1½ teaspoons minced Italian parsley

1 tablespoon freshly grated Parmigiano-Reggiano cheese

12 large sea scallops (about 1 pound), feet removed

Kosher salt and freshly ground black pepper

3 tablespoons extra-virgin olive oil

¼ cup diced yellow onion

4 ounces button mushrooms, sliced

¼ cup white wine

¾ cup heavy cream

1 teaspoon minced fresh thyme

Several drops of truffle oil (optional), to your taste

Preheat the oven to 375°F. Toss the bread crumbs with the melted butter in a medium-size bowl, making sure that the bread crumbs are evenly coated. Spread on a baking sheet and bake, stirring once or twice, for 7 to 8 minutes, or until toasted and golden brown. Let cool and add the parsley and Parmigiano-Reggiano cheese.

Gently pat the scallops dry with paper towels. Season them generously with salt and pepper and set aside at room temperature for about 30 minutes.

Heat a large, heavy sauté pan over high heat until very hot but not smoking. Add the oil and swirl to coat the bottom of the pan. Add the scallops and cook without disturbing for 2 to 3 minutes, or until they release from the pan and are crusty and brown. Using tongs, turn the scallops over and continue to cook over high heat for another 1 to 2 minutes, or until they reach the desired doneness. Moisture will just begin to accumulate on the surface of the scallops when they are medium-rare. Remove the scallops to a plate and tent with foil to keep warm.

Reduce the heat to medium; add the onion, mushrooms, and a generous pinch of salt to the pan; and sauté for 2 to 3 minutes, or until the vegetables are soft. Add the wine and simmer for a minute or so, scraping up the browned bits from the bottom of the pan with a heatproof spatula. Add the cream and thyme and simmer for another 3 to 4 minutes, or until the sauce is thickened. Remove the pan from the heat, stir in the truffle oil (if using) and any accumulated juices from the scallops, and season with salt and pepper to taste.

Spoon some of the sauce into the center of each of four plates. Arrange 3 scallops atop each pool of sauce and sprinkle with the seasoned bread crumbs. Serve immediately.

scallops with carrot-ginger emulsion

Light rather than extra-virgin olive oil is used in this recipe so that the flavors of the carrot and ginger come through loud and clear. Fresh carrot juice, which is available at most juice bars and supermarkets, is the best choice for the sauce. Bottled pure pressed carrot juice also yields good results; look for it in the refrigerated section at natural foods or health food stores. Serve these scallops with basmati rice or fluffy couscous.   Serves 4

12 large sea scallops (about 1 pound), feet removed

Kosher salt and freshly ground black pepper

2 cups carrot juice

1 tablespoon grated fresh ginger

1 tablespoon honey

1 teaspoon freshly squeezed lime juice

6 tablespoons light olive oil

1 tablespoon minced fresh cilantro

Gently pat the scallops dry with paper towels. Season them generously with salt and pepper and set aside at room temperature for about 30 minutes.

Combine the carrot juice, ginger, honey, and lime juice in a small saucepan. Bring to a boil and simmer for 30 to 35 minutes, or until reduced to about ½ cup. Transfer to a blender and, with the motor running, add 3 tablespoons of the oil in a thin stream. Process until the oil is incorporated. Season with salt and pepper to taste.

Heat a large, heavy sauté pan over high heat until very hot but not smoking. Add the remaining 3 tablespoons oil and swirl to coat the bottom of the pan. Add the scallops and cook without disturbing for 2 to 3 minutes, or until they release from the pan and are crusty and brown. Using tongs, turn the scallops over and continue to cook over high heat for another 1 to 2 minutes, or until they reach the desired doneness. Moisture will just begin to accumulate on the surface of the scallops when they are medium-rare.

Arrange the scallops on individual plates, divide the sauce among the scallops, sprinkle with the cilantro, and serve immediately.

scallops with champagne sauce and salmon roe

The decadent pairing of scallops and caviar is made even better with a silky sauce splashed with Champagne. These ingredients may sound extravagant, but salmon roe, which is available at European delis and most gourmet grocers, is relatively inexpensive, and any affordable sparkling wine, such as cava or Prosecco, can stand in for the Champagne. Serve the dish with a glass of bubbly.

Serves 4

Gently pat the scallops dry with paper towels. Season them generously with salt and pepper and set aside at room temperature for about 30 minutes.

Heat a large, heavy sauté pan over high heat until very hot but not smoking. Add the oil and swirl to coat the bottom of the pan. Add the scallops and cook without disturbing for 2 to 3 minutes, or until they release from the pan and are crusty and brown. Using tongs, turn the scallops over and continue to cook over high heat for another 1 to 2 minutes, or until they reach the desired doneness. Moisture will just begin to accumulate on the surface of the scallops when they are medium-rare. Remove the scallops to a plate and tent with foil to keep warm.

Reduce the heat to medium, add the Champagne to the pan, and simmer for a minute or so, scraping up the browned bits from the bottom of the pan with a heatproof spatula. Add the cream and simmer for another 2 to 3 minutes, or until the sauce is thickened. Remove the pan from the heat; stir in the sour cream, chives, dill, and any accumulated juices from the scallops, and season with salt and pepper to taste.

Spoon some of the sauce into the center of each of four plates. Arrange 3 scallops atop each pool of sauce and top with a tablespoonful of the salmon roe. Serve immediately.

12 large sea scallops (about 1 pound), feet removed

Kosher salt and freshly ground black pepper

2 tablespoons extra-virgin olive oil

¼ cup Champagne

¾ cup heavy cream

2 tablespoons sour cream or crème fraîche

1 tablespoon minced fresh chives

1 tablespoon minced fresh dill

¼ cup salmon roe

ginger-orange-soy–glazed salmon fillets

Refreshing and light, these salmon fillets have an Asian flair. I use a Microplane, which I prefer to a garlic press, to grate garlic for recipes where a mince would be too coarse. I use the root end of the garlic as a little "handle." Accompany the salmon with Rice Noodle Salad (page 138) or a vegetable stir-fry.

Serves 4

3 tablespoons soy sauce

3 tablespoons honey

1 teaspoon grated orange zest

Juice of 1 orange

1 teaspoon grated fresh ginger

1 clove garlic, grated

Generous pinch of red pepper flakes, or to taste

Several drops of dark sesame oil, to your taste

4 salmon fillets, preferably Chinook or king (page 90), weighing about 6 ounces each, skinned and boned

Kosher salt and freshly ground black pepper

2 tablespoons canola oil

2 tablespoons sliced green onions

1 tablespoon sesame seeds, toasted

Combine the soy sauce, honey, zest, orange juice, ginger, garlic, and red pepper flakes in a small saucepan. Bring to a boil and simmer for 5 to 6 minutes, or until very thick and syrupy. Remove from the heat and stir in the sesame oil.

Season the fillets generously with salt and pepper and set aside at room temperature for about 30 minutes.

Heat a large, heavy sauté pan over high heat until very hot but not smoking. Add the canola oil and swirl to coat the bottom of the pan. Add the fillets, skinned side up, and cook without disturbing for 4 to 5 minutes, or until they release from the pan and are crusty and brown. Very gently, with a flexible fish spatula, turn the fillets over and continue to cook over high heat for another 2 to 3 minutes, or until they reach the desired doneness. Brush the fillets with the glaze during the last minute of cooking. The fillets will barely begin to flake when they are medium-rare.

Arrange the fillets on individual plates, brush with additional glaze, sprinkle with the green onions and sesame seeds, and serve immediately.

porcini-crusted salmon fillets

Dried porcini mushrooms can be ground to a fine powder and used just like a spice rub on beef, pork, lamb, and duck as well as salmon. Accompany these salmon fillets with steamed asparagus and Truffled Mashed Potatoes (page 134).

Serves 4

Grind the dried porcinis to a fine powder in a blender, spice mill, or clean coffee grinder. Season the fillets generously with salt and pepper and coat with the porcini powder. Set aside at room temperature for about 30 minutes.

Heat a large, heavy sauté pan over medium-high heat until very hot but not smoking. Add the oil and swirl to coat the bottom of the pan. Add the fillets, skinned side up, and cook without disturbing for 4 to 5 minutes, or until they release from the pan and are crusty and brown. Very gently, with a flexible fish spatula, turn the fillets over and continue to cook over medium-high heat for another 2 to 3 minutes, or until they reach the desired doneness. The fillets will barely begin to flake when they are medium-rare. Remove the fillets to a plate and tent with foil to keep warm.

Reduce the heat to medium, add the shallot to the pan, and sauté for 30 seconds, or until translucent and fragrant. Add the lemon juice and thyme and simmer for a minute or so, scraping up the browned bits from the bottom of the pan with a heatproof spatula. Remove the pan from the heat and let cool for a minute or two. Whisk in the butter quickly, stir in any accumulated juices from the fillets, and season with salt and pepper to taste.

Arrange the fillets on individual plates, divide the sauce among the fillets, and serve immediately.

½ ounce dried porcini mushrooms

4 salmon fillets, preferably Chinook or king (page 90), weighing about 6 ounces each, skinned and boned

Kosher salt and freshly ground black pepper

2 tablespoons extra-virgin olive oil

1 shallot, minced

2 tablespoons freshly squeezed lemon juice

½ teaspoon minced fresh thyme

3 tablespoons cold unsalted butter, diced

chile-rubbed salmon with mango salsa

This colorful dish is sophisticated enough for a dinner party, yet simple enough for a weeknight dinner. The chile rub is versatile; it's great on everything from steak to chops to shrimp. Make a large batch and keep it on hand.

Serves 4

2 large ripe mangoes, peeled and diced

2 Roma tomatoes, seeded and diced

½ medium-size red onion, diced

½ red bell pepper, seeded and diced

1 to 2 jalapeño chiles, seeded and diced, to your taste

¼ cup minced fresh cilantro

2 tablespoons freshly squeezed lime juice

Kosher salt

3 tablespoons pure chile powder (page 22)

1½ teaspoons light brown sugar

1 teaspoon ground cumin

1 teaspoon granulated garlic

4 salmon fillets, preferably Chinook or king (page 90), weighing about 6 ounces each, skinned and boned

2 tablespoons canola oil

Combine the mangoes, tomatoes, onion, bell pepper, jalapeños, cilantro, and lime juice in a medium-size bowl. Season with salt to taste and let macerate at room temperature for 1 to 2 hours.

Combine the chile powder, brown sugar, cumin, and granulated garlic in a small bowl. Season the fillets generously with salt and coat with the chile powder blend. Set aside at room temperature for about 30 minutes.

Heat a large, heavy sauté pan over medium-high heat until very hot but not smoking. Add the oil and swirl to coat the bottom of the pan. Add the fillets, skinned side up, and cook without disturbing for 4 to 5 minutes, or until they release from the pan and are crusty and brown. Very gently, with a flexible fish spatula, turn the fillets over and continue to cook over medium-high heat for another 2 to 3 minutes, or until they reach the desired doneness. The fillets will barely begin to flake when they are medium-rare.

Arrange the fillets on individual plates, divide the salsa among the fillets, and serve immediately.

salmon fillets with green peppercorn sauce

Black, white, and green peppercorns are all products of the same plant but are harvested at different points of ripeness and processed in different ways. Green peppercorns, which are available either dried or packed in brine, have the most herbaceous flavor and are the least pungent of the three.

Serves 4

Season the fillets generously with salt and pepper and set aside at room temperature for about 30 minutes.

Heat a large, heavy sauté pan over high heat until very hot but not smoking. Add the oil and swirl to coat the bottom of the pan. Add the fillets, skinned side up, and cook without disturbing for 4 to 5 minutes, or until they release from the pan and are crusty and brown. Very gently, with a flexible fish spatula, turn the fillets over and continue to cook over high heat for another 2 to 3 minutes, or until they reach the desired doneness. The fillets will barely begin to flake when they are medium-rare. Remove the fillets to a plate and tent with foil to keep warm.

Reduce the heat to medium, add the shallot to the pan, and sauté for 30 seconds, or until translucent and fragrant. Add the wine and simmer for a minute or so, scraping up the browned bits from the bottom of the pan with a heatproof spatula. Add the cream and peppercorns and simmer for another 2 to 3 minutes, or until the sauce is thickened. Stir in any accumulated juices from the fillets and season with salt to taste.

Arrange the fillets on individual plates, divide the sauce among the fillets, and serve immediately.

4 salmon fillets, preferably Chinook or king (page 90), weighing about 6 ounces each, skinned and boned

Kosher salt and freshly ground black pepper

2 tablespoons extra-virgin olive oil

1 shallot, minced

¼ cup white wine

½ cup heavy cream

2 teaspoons green peppercorns in brine, drained and crushed

thyme-infused salmon fillets

This simple recipe allows the flavor of the salmon to shine. I created it for my father, a very picky eater who insists that sauces are not worth eating.

Serves 4

4 salmon fillets, preferably Chinook or king (below), weighing about 6 ounces each, skinned and boned

Kosher salt and freshly ground black pepper

4 sprigs fresh thyme

2 tablespoons extra-virgin olive oil

Lemon wedges for garnish

Season the fillets generously with salt and pepper and press 1 thyme sprig into the flesh side of each fillet. Set aside at room temperature for about 30 minutes.

Heat a large, heavy sauté pan over high heat until very hot but not smoking. Add the oil and swirl to coat the bottom of the pan. Add the fillets, skinned side up, and cook without disturbing for 4 to 5 minutes, or until they release from the pan and are crusty and brown. Very gently, with a flexible fish spatula, turn the fillets over and continue to cook over high heat for another 2 to 3 minutes, or until they reach the desired doneness. The fillets will barely begin to flake when they are medium-rare.

Arrange the fillets on individual plates, garnish with the lemon wedges, and serve immediately.

selecting salmon

Chinook, or king, salmon, with its high fat content, full flavor, and firm, thick flesh, is the tastiest salmon on the market. If Chinook salmon is unavailable or too pricey, use Atlantic salmon. The thickness of Chinook and Atlantic salmon fillets, which can reach 1½ inches or more, makes them particularly well suited to searing; they brown nicely and remain succulent within. If all you can find are coho or sockeye salmon, which are small and have relatively thin fillets, opt for steaks rather than fillets. No matter what variety of salmon you choose, ask for the thickest center-cut pieces, and if you don't want to skin and bone the fish yourself, your fishmonger will be happy to do it for you.

salmon fillets with green tea sauce

Matcha is the powdered green tea traditionally used in the Japanese tea ceremony. It has a brilliant green color and slightly sweet vegetal flavor that complements both sweet and savory dishes. Matcha can be found at tea shops and many Asian markets. Steamed Baby Bok Choy (page 141) and soba noodles with sliced shiitake mushrooms and a dash of soy sauce are the perfect accompaniments to this dish.

Serves 4

Combine the soy sauce, garlic, and ginger in a large zipper-top plastic bag. Add the fillets and turn to coat. Seal the bag, letting out all the air. Marinate the fillets for about 2 hours in the refrigerator.

Remove the fillets from the marinade and set aside at room temperature for about 30 minutes. Discard the marinade.

Pat the fillets dry with paper towels. Heat a large, heavy sauté pan over high heat until very hot but not smoking. Add the oil and swirl to coat the bottom of the pan. Add the fillets, skinned side up, and cook without disturbing for 4 to 5 minutes, or until they release from the pan and are crusty and brown. Very gently, with a flexible fish spatula, turn the fillets over and continue to cook over high heat for another 2 to 3 minutes, or until they reach the desired doneness. The fillets will barely begin to flake when they are medium-rare. Remove the fillets to a plate and tent with foil to keep warm.

Add the sake to the pan and simmer for a minute or so, scraping up the browned bits from the bottom of the pan with a heatproof spatula. Add the broth and cream and simmer for another 2 to 3 minutes, or until the sauce is thickened. Remove the pan from the heat and whisk in the matcha and sugar. Strain the sauce into a bowl through a fine-mesh sieve, stir in any accumulated juices from the fillets, and season with salt.

Arrange the fillets on individual plates, divide the sauce among the fillets, sprinkle with the sesame seeds and green onions, and serve immediately.

2 tablespoons soy sauce

1 clove garlic, crushed

1 teaspoon grated fresh ginger

4 salmon fillets, preferably Chinook or king (page 90), weighing about 6 ounces each, skinned and boned

2 tablespoons canola oil

¼ cup sake

¼ cup chicken broth

½ cup heavy cream

1 tablespoon matcha

½ teaspoon sugar

Kosher salt to taste

1 tablespoon sesame seeds, toasted

2 tablespoons sliced green onions

halibut with salsa verde

Salsa verde, a traditional Italian condiment served with simply prepared meat, poultry, or vegetables, has a touch of anchovy that accents the flavor of seared fish fillets.

Serves 4

Four 1-inch-thick halibut fillets, weighing about 6 ounces each, skinned and boned

Kosher salt and freshly ground black pepper

1 cup Italian parsley

1 shallot, diced

1 tablespoon capers

2 anchovy fillets

¼ cup plus 3 tablespoons extra-virgin olive oil

Season the fillets generously with salt and pepper. Set aside at room temperature for about 30 minutes.

Combine the parsley, shallot, capers, anchovies, and ¼ cup of the oil in a food processor and pulse until smooth. Season with salt and pepper to taste.

Heat a large, heavy sauté pan over high heat until very hot but not smoking. Add the remaining 3 tablespoons oil and swirl to coat the bottom of the pan. Add the fillets, skinned side up, and cook without disturbing for 4 to 5 minutes, or until they release from the pan and are crusty and brown. Very gently, with a flexible fish spatula, turn the fillets over and continue to cook over high heat for another 2 to 3 minutes, or until they are just cooked through. The fillets will begin to flake at this point.

Arrange the fillets on individual plates, divide the salsa among the fillets, and serve immediately.

how to roast bell peppers and chiles

Homemade roasted peppers and chiles have a most delicious campfire character. They are far superior to jarred roasted peppers in both flavor and texture. Select straight-sided peppers; irregularly shaped ones are difficult to roast evenly. Place the whole pepper directly on the grate of a gas burner and set the heat to high, so that the flame licks the pepper. If you don't have a gas stove, use the broiler. Cook the pepper, using tongs to turn it, for 1 to 2 minutes per side, until the skin is charred and blistered all over. The flesh of the pepper will still be firm. Transfer the pepper to a bowl, seal the bowl with plastic wrap, and set it aside for about 15 minutes, or until the pepper is cool enough to handle. The steam from the pepper will finish the cooking process and loosen the skin. Once the pepper is cool, use a paring knife to scrape off the skin—don't worry about removing every last black speck—and then seed it. This technique can be used to roast green, red, yellow, or orange bell peppers and chiles such as Anaheims and poblanos. Roasted peppers will keep in a tightly sealed container in the refrigerator for up to 3 days.

halibut with
roasted red pepper coulis

A brightly colored and flavored sauce made from pureed vegetables or fruit is known as a coulis. Homemade roasted bell peppers are essential for this coulis; do not use jarred peppers, as they have an acidic flavor and limp texture. For a different color and slight flavor variation, substitute a yellow or orange pepper for the red. Serve the dish with Parmesan orzo and sautéed broccolini.

Serves 4

Season the fillets generously with salt and pepper. Set aside at room temperature for about 30 minutes. Combine the bell pepper and broth in a blender and process until smooth.

Heat a large, heavy sauté pan over high heat until very hot but not smoking. Add the oil and swirl to coat the bottom of the pan. Add the fillets, skinned side up, and cook without disturbing for 4 to 5 minutes, or until they release from the pan and are crusty and brown. Very gently, with a flexible fish spatula, turn the fillets over and continue to cook over high heat for another 2 to 3 minutes, or until they are just cooked through. The fillets will begin to flake at this point. Remove the fillets to a plate and tent with foil to keep warm.

Reduce the heat to medium, add the garlic to the pan, and sauté for 30 seconds, or until fragrant. Add the wine and simmer for a minute or so, scraping up the browned bits from the bottom of the pan with a heatproof spatula. Add the bell pepper mixture and simmer for another 2 to 3 minutes, or until the sauce is thickened. Stir in the lemon juice and any accumulated juices from the fillets and season with salt and pepper to taste.

Arrange the fillets on individual plates, divide the coulis among the fillets, and serve immediately.

Four 1-inch-thick halibut fillets, weighing about 6 ounces each, skinned and boned

Kosher salt and freshly ground black pepper

1 roasted red bell pepper (page 92)

½ cup chicken broth

2 tablespoons extra-virgin olive oil

1 clove garlic, minced

¼ cup white wine

½ teaspoon freshly squeezed lemon juice

sesame-crusted tuna steaks

Perennially popular in restaurants, seared rare tuna with a crunchy crust of sesame seeds can easily be made at home. Serve this dish with Rice Noodle Salad (page 138), and, if you like, offer a bit of wasabi.

Serves 4

Four 1¼- to 1½-inch-thick tuna steaks, preferably ahi (page 97), weighing about 6 ounces each

Kosher salt and freshly ground black pepper

2 tablespoons white sesame seeds

2 tablespoons black sesame seeds

2 tablespoons canola oil

½ cup sake

2 teaspoons sugar

½ teaspoon grated fresh ginger

1 tablespoon soy sauce

Several drops of dark sesame oil, to your taste

1 tablespoon sliced green onions

Season the steaks generously with salt and pepper and set aside at room temperature for about 30 minutes. Combine the white and black sesame seeds in a small bowl. Coat the steaks with the sesame seeds, pressing them gently into the fish.

Heat a large, heavy sauté pan over high heat until very hot but not smoking. Add the oil and swirl to coat the bottom of the pan. Add the steaks and cook without disturbing for 1 to 2 minutes, or until they release from the pan and are crusty and brown. Very gently, with a flexible fish spatula, turn the steaks over and continue to cook over high heat for another 1 to 2 minutes, or until they reach the desired doneness. The steaks will be soft to the touch when they are rare. Remove the steaks to a plate and tent with foil to keep warm.

Reduce the heat to medium; add the sake, sugar, and ginger to the pan; and simmer, scraping up the browned bits from the bottom of the pan with a heatproof spatula, for 2 to 3 minutes, or until the sauce is thickened and slightly syrupy. Remove the pan from the heat and stir in the soy sauce, sesame oil, green onions, and any accumulated juices from the steaks.

Arrange the steaks on individual plates, divide the sauce among the steaks, and serve immediately.

herbed tuna and white bean salad

Fresh tuna replaces canned oil-packed tuna in this version of the traditional Italian salad. Feel free to vary the herbs in the recipe; basil, thyme, oregano, or tarragon would be just as delicious as rosemary. Served on a bed of mesclun greens or butter lettuce, along with some rustic bread, this salad makes a hearty lunch or light supper. **Serves 4**

Season the steaks generously with salt and pepper and set aside at room temperature for about 30 minutes.

Whisk together the vinegar, mustard, rosemary, and parsley in a medium-size bowl. Continue whisking while adding ½ cup of the oil in a thin stream. Combine the beans, tomatoes, and onion in a large bowl. Add all but about 2 tablespoons of the vinaigrette and stir to combine. Season with salt and pepper to taste.

Heat a large, heavy sauté pan over high heat until very hot but not smoking. Add the remaining 2 tablespoons oil and swirl to coat the bottom of the pan. Add the steaks and cook without disturbing for 1 to 2 minutes, or until they release from the pan and are crusty and brown. Very gently, with a flexible fish spatula, turn the steaks over and continue to cook over high heat for another 1 to 2 minutes, or until they reach the desired doneness. The steaks will be soft to the touch when they are rare. Remove the steaks to a plate and tent with foil to keep warm.

Spoon a portion of the bean mixture into the center of each of four plates. Slice the steaks thinly and fan out the slices atop each mound of beans. Drizzle with the remaining 2 tablespoons vinaigrette and serve immediately.

Four 1¼- to 1½-inch-thick tuna steaks, preferably ahi (page 97), weighing about 6 ounces each

Kosher salt and freshly ground black pepper

3 tablespoons red wine vinegar

2 teaspoons Dijon mustard

1 tablespoon minced fresh rosemary

1 tablespoon minced Italian parsley

½ cup plus 2 tablespoons extra-virgin olive oil

Two 15-ounce cans cannellini beans, rinsed and drained

2 cups cherry tomatoes, halved

¾ cup finely diced red onion

seared tuna salad niçoise

This composed salad is as colorful as it is delicious. The classic French version is made with canned oil-packed tuna, but modern interpretations like this one frequently opt for seared fresh tuna instead. Haricots verts, which are French green beans, are very slender and more tender than other varieties. They are often available at gourmet grocers and farmers' markets. If you cannot obtain them, use the smallest green beans you can find. Serve this salad with plenty of crusty bread.   Serves 4

Four 1¼- to 1½-inch-thick tuna steaks, preferably ahi (page 97), weighing about 6 ounces each

Kosher salt and freshly ground black pepper

8 fingerling potatoes

3 tablespoons red wine vinegar

1 shallot, minced

1 tablespoon minced Italian parsley

2 teaspoons Dijon mustard

1 teaspoon minced fresh thyme

½ cup plus 2 tablespoons extra-virgin olive oil

8 ounces haricots verts, ends trimmed

1 cup cherry tomatoes, halved

1 head butter lettuce, leaves separated

2 hard-cooked eggs

½ cup niçoise olives

Season the steaks generously with salt and pepper and set aside at room temperature for about 30 minutes.

Place the potatoes in a medium-size saucepan and add enough water to cover by several inches. Add several large pinches of salt. Bring to a boil and simmer for 10 to 12 minutes, or until tender. Whisk together the vinegar, shallot, parsley, mustard, and thyme in a medium-size bowl. Continue whisking while adding ½ cup of the oil in a thin stream. Season with salt and pepper to taste. Drain the potatoes when they are tender, cut them into quarters, and toss with enough vinaigrette to coat.

Meanwhile, bring a medium-size saucepan of water to a rolling boil. Add the haricots verts and several large pinches of salt. Boil for 5 to 6 minutes, or until tender. Drain the haricots verts and immediately dunk into a large bowl of ice water. Drain well.

Heat a large, heavy sauté pan over high heat until very hot but not smoking. Add the remaining 2 tablespoons oil and swirl to coat the bottom of the pan. Add the steaks and cook without disturbing for 1 to 2 minutes, or until they release from the pan and are crusty and brown. Very gently, with a flexible fish spatula, turn the steaks over and continue to cook over high heat for another 1 to 2 minutes, or until they reach the desired doneness. The steaks will be soft to the touch when they are rare. Remove the steaks to a plate and tent with foil to keep warm.

In separate bowls, toss the haricots verts, tomatoes, and lettuce with enough vinaigrette to coat. Quarter the eggs.

Mound the lettuce on a platter. Slice the steaks thinly. Arrange the potatoes, haricots verts, tomatoes, olives, eggs, and tuna slices decoratively atop the lettuce. Drizzle with the remaining vinaigrette and serve immediately.

selecting and cooking tuna

Bigeye and yellowfin are the best varieties of tuna for searing rare, and the term *ahi* can refer to either one. The meat of the bigeye tuna has a high fat content, red color, bold flavor, and meaty texture. Yellowfin tuna is deep pink and moist with a slightly lower fat content than bigeye. Albacore, or tombo, tuna has pale pink and mildly flavored lean flesh and is the only tuna that can be considered a "white" fish. It is suitable for searing and also widely available canned. The dark red meat of the bluefin tuna, which has the highest fat content of all of the tuna varieties, is highly prized, and almost all of it is exported to Japan, where it is eaten as sushi or sashimi. It is expensive and difficult to find, and although it would certainly taste great seared, it is best enjoyed raw.

No matter what type of tuna you choose to sear, select the freshest steaks available. Trim off any dark red blood lines, which have an unappetizing color and strong flavor, before cooking. Sear the tuna very quickly in a very hot pan just until rare. Watch it carefully to avoid overcooking; thoroughly cooked tuna is pale and dry and tastes like it came out of a can. For a restaurant-style presentation, cut the seared tuna into thin slices and fan out the pieces on plates. The dramatic contrast between tuna's seared surface and rare center is visually appreciated when the slices overlap slightly.

tuna with meyer lemon emulsion

This dish is a celebration of the sweet and intoxicatingly aromatic Meyer lemon, which appears in markets only during the winter months. Lemon lovers will also enjoy this puckery sauce served over shrimp, scallops, halibut, and even asparagus. The Meyer is used in three forms here—zest for flavor, juice for acidity, and suprêmes for texture. Zest the lemons first. It's much easier to remove the zest from a whole fruit than from a piece of rind. A Microplane yields the best results, but you can also use a zester or fine grater. Cut the suprêmes next, since you will definitely get some juice in the process. Measure this juice and squeeze more lemons until you have the necessary ¼ cup. Be sure to add the lemon juice to the cream mixture slowly so that the acid does not cause the cream to curdle. You will need about three large Meyer lemons for this recipe. Serves 4

Four 1¼- to 1½-inch-thick tuna steaks, preferably ahi (page 97), weighing about 6 ounces each

Kosher salt and freshly ground black pepper

2 tablespoons heavy cream

1 teaspoon grated Meyer lemon zest

1 teaspoon sugar

¼ cup freshly squeezed Meyer lemon juice

4 to 6 tablespoons extra-virgin olive oil

Suprêmes from 2 Meyer lemons (page 99)

Season the steaks generously with salt and pepper and set aside at room temperature for about 30 minutes.

Combine the cream, zest, and sugar in a small saucepan. Slowly add the lemon juice while whisking. Bring to a boil and simmer for 5 to 6 minutes, or until reduced to about 2 tablespoons. Transfer to a blender and, with the motor running, add 2 table-spoons of the oil (or up to 4 tablespoons, to your taste) in a thin stream. Process until the oil is incorporated. Transfer to a bowl, gently fold in the suprêmes, and season with salt and pepper to taste.

Heat a large, heavy sauté pan over high heat until very hot but not smoking. Add the remaining 2 tablespoons oil and swirl to coat the bottom of the pan. Add the steaks and cook with-out disturbing for 1 to 2 minutes, or until they release from the pan and are crusty and brown. Very gently, with a flexible fish spatula, turn the steaks over and continue to cook over high heat for another 1 to 2 minutes, or until they reach the desired doneness. The steaks will be soft to the touch when they are rare.

Arrange the steaks on individual plates, divide the emulsion among the steaks, and serve immediately.

suprêmes

A segment of citrus fruit minus membranes and seeds is known as a suprême. These pieces of fruit have a great texture and look like little jewels. Orange (especially blood orange), grapefruit, tangerine, lemon, and lime suprêmes make great garnishes for sauces, salads, and desserts.

To make suprêmes, use a very sharp knife to cut the ends off a piece of citrus fruit. Stand the fruit on one cut end and cut the rind away from the flesh in narrow strips, removing all of the white pith and as little of the flesh as possible, until the fruit is naked. Then, working over a bowl to catch any juice, slowly and carefully cut each segment from between the membranes and gently pick out any seeds from the segments. Squeeze the membranes for any remaining juice.

mahi-mahi with spicy sweet and sour glaze

Mahi-mahi, a tropical fish with firm-textured flesh and a light flavor, is often served with sweet, fruity sauces, such as this one. Fish sauce can be found at Asian markets, gourmet grocers, and many supermarkets. I accompany this dish with Rice Noodle Salad (page 138).

Serves 4

Four 1-inch-thick mahi-mahi fillets, weighing about 6 ounces each, skinned and boned

Kosher salt and freshly ground black pepper

½ cup freshly squeezed lime juice

½ cup light brown sugar

½ cup diced pineapple

1 red Thai chile, seeded and minced

1 clove garlic, grated

2 tablespoons sliced green onions

2 tablespoons fish sauce

2 tablespoons canola oil

Season the fillets generously with salt and pepper and set aside at room temperature for about 30 minutes.

Combine the lime juice, brown sugar, pineapple, chile, garlic, and green onions in a small saucepan. Bring to a boil and simmer for 6 to 7 minutes, or until the sauce is slightly thickened and syrupy. Remove from the heat and stir in the fish sauce.

Heat a large, heavy sauté pan over high heat until very hot but not smoking. Add the oil and swirl to coat the bottom of the pan. Add the fillets, skinned side up, and cook without disturbing for 4 to 5 minutes, or until they release from the pan and are crusty and brown. Very gently, with a flexible fish spatula, turn the fillets over and continue to cook over high heat for another 3 to 4 minutes, or until they are just cooked through. The fillets will begin to flake at this point.

Arrange the fillets on individual plates, divide the glaze among the fillets, and serve immediately.

swordfish with tangy cucumber salad

A light, refreshingly crisp cucumber salad is a delicious topping for meaty swordfish. The salad is actually a quick pickle, and the secret to its crunch is tossing the cucumber slices with salt to draw out as much water as possible. Salmon fillets are a fine substitute if swordfish is unavailable. For a bento-style meal, serve this dish with sticky rice. **Serves 4**

Combine the sake, 2 tablespoons of the soy sauce, honey, and ginger in a large zipper-top plastic bag. Add the steaks and turn to coat. Seal the bag, letting out all the air. Marinate the steaks for about 2 hours in the refrigerator.

Toss the cucumber with the salt in a colander and let drain for 16 to 20 minutes. Transfer to a clean dishtowel, gather the corners together, and squeeze to remove any extra moisture from the cucumber. In a large bowl toss together the cucumber, garlic, chile, vinegar, sugar, and remaining 1 tablespoon soy sauce.

Remove the steaks from the marinade and set aside at room temperature for about 30 minutes. Discard the marinade.

Pat the steaks dry with paper towels. Heat a large, heavy sauté pan over medium-high heat until very hot but not smoking. Add the oil and swirl to coat the bottom of the pan. Add the steaks and cook without disturbing for 3 to 4 minutes, or until they release from the pan and are crusty and brown. Very gently, with a flexible fish spatula, turn the fillets over and continue to cook over medium-high heat for another 2 to 3 minutes, or until they are just cooked through. The fillets will begin to flake at this point.

Arrange the fillets on individual plates, divide the salad among the fillets, and serve immediately.

2 tablespoons sake

3 tablespoons soy sauce

2 tablespoons honey

1 teaspoon grated fresh ginger

Four 1- to 1¼-inch-thick swordfish steaks, weighing about 6 ounces each, skinned and boned

1 English cucumber, thinly sliced

1 teaspoon kosher salt

1 clove garlic, grated

1 red Thai chile, seeded and minced

2 tablespoons unseasoned rice vinegar

1 tablespoon sugar

2 tablespoons canola oil

prosciutto-wrapped monkfish
with lemon-butter sauce

Monkfish fillets and prosciutto is a favorite combination of mine, as the salty ham brings out the delicate sweetness of the fish. The fillets have a sort of triangular shape, so they are seared on all three sides. Be sure to have the prosciutto sliced slightly thicker than usual—paper-thin prosciutto will disintegrate in the pan.   Serves 4

4 monkfish fillets, weighing about 8 ounces each

Kosher salt and freshly ground black pepper

8 slices prosciutto

2 tablespoons extra-virgin olive oil

2 cloves garlic, minced

2 tablespoons freshly squeezed lemon juice

½ teaspoon grated lemon zest

¼ cup (½ stick) cold unsalted butter, diced

Season the fillets generously with salt and pepper. Wrap 2 slices prosciutto around each fillet. Set aside at room temperature for about 30 minutes. Preheat the oven to 450°F.

Heat a large, heavy, ovenproof sauté pan over medium-high heat until very hot but not smoking. Add the oil and swirl to coat the bottom of the pan. Add the fillets, broad side down, and cook without disturbing for 2 to 3 minutes, or until they release from the pan and are crusty and brown. Very gently, with a flexible fish spatula, turn the fillets onto another side and cook for 2 to 3 minutes more. Turn the fillets onto the third side, transfer the pan to the oven, and roast the fillets for 14 to 16 minutes, or until they are just cooked through. The fillets will begin to flake at this point. Remove the fillets to a plate and tent with foil to keep warm.

Set the pan over medium heat, add the garlic to the pan, and sauté for 30 seconds, or until translucent and fragrant. Add the lemon juice and zest and simmer for a minute or so, scraping up the browned bits from the bottom of the pan with a heat-proof spatula. Remove the pan from the heat and let cool for a minute or two. Whisk in the butter quickly, stir in any accumulated juices from the fillets, and season with salt and pepper to taste.

Cut the fillets into ½-inch-thick slices. Arrange the slices on individual plates, divide the sauce among the slices, and serve immediately.

bronzed fish fillets

The Louisiana tradition of blackened redfish inspired me to create this recipe. Blackening is a cooking technique in which an item, such as a fish fillet or steak, is coated in butter and spices and cooked very quickly in an insanely hot cast-iron skillet. The result is a succulent dish with a delicious smoky crust. Unfortunately, the fire hazard makes it a rather inaccessible cooking method for the home cook; the butter is sure to flare up when it hits the hot pan and create dramatic black clouds of cayenne-laced smoke. I learned this years ago when I ignored all of the warnings and attempted the technique in my apartment kitchen. In subsequent efforts, I opened all the windows, disarmed the fire alarm, sent my husband outside, and wrapped a towel around my face to protect me from the imminent coughing fit. Eventually I managed to devise this far simpler and safer method. Redfish is the most common choice for blackening, but any firm-fleshed fish can be used for this recipe. Snapper, catfish, and tilapia fillets are delicious when prepared this way. Also try tuna steaks, which should be left rare, or salmon fillets. Serve with garlic butter (page 33) and a sprinkling of minced Italian parsley.

Serves 4

Combine the granulated garlic, onion powder, paprika, black pepper, thyme, oregano, and cayenne in a small bowl. Season the fillets generously with salt and coat with the spice blend. Set aside at room temperature for about 30 minutes.

Heat a large, heavy sauté pan over high heat until very hot but not smoking. Add the oil and swirl to coat the bottom of the pan. Add the fillets, skinned side up, and cook without disturbing for 2 to 3 minutes, or until they release from the pan and are crusty and brown. Very gently, with a flexible fish spatula, turn the fillets over and continue to cook over high heat for another 1 to 2 minutes, or until they are just cooked through. The fillets will begin to flake at this point.

Arrange the fillets on individual plates, garnish with the lemon wedges, and serve immediately.

1 teaspoon granulated garlic

1 teaspoon onion powder

1 teaspoon paprika

1 teaspoon freshly ground black pepper

½ teaspoon dried thyme leaves

½ teaspoon dried oregano

½ teaspoon cayenne pepper

4 firm-fleshed fish fillets, weighing about 6 ounces each, skinned and boned

Kosher salt

3 tablespoons canola oil

Lemon wedges for garnish

trout amandine

When a recipe calls for dressed fish or fowl, it means nothing more than that it has been prepared for cooking. In this case, the trout should be gutted, with the head on or off as you prefer.

Serves 4

4 trout, weighing about 8 ounces each, dressed

Kosher salt and freshly ground black pepper

3 tablespoons extra-virgin olive oil

6 tablespoons (¾ stick) unsalted butter, diced

1 shallot, minced

¼ cup sliced almonds, toasted

1 tablespoon minced Italian parsley

Lemon wedges for garnish

Season the trout generously with salt and pepper, inside and out, and set aside at room temperature for about 30 minutes.

Heat a very large, heavy sauté pan over medium-high heat until very hot but not smoking. Add the oil and swirl to coat the bottom of the pan. Add the trout and cook without disturbing for 4 to 5 minutes, or until they release from the pan and are crusty and brown. Very gently, with a flexible fish spatula, turn the trout over and continue to cook over medium-high heat for another 2 to 3 minutes, or until cooked through. The trout will just begin to flake at this point. Remove the trout to a plate and tent with foil to keep warm.

Reduce the heat to medium, add the butter to the pan, and cook for 3 to 4 minutes, or until browned. Add the shallot to the pan and sauté for 30 seconds, or until translucent and fragrant. Remove the pan from the heat, stir in the almonds and parsley, and season with salt and pepper to taste.

Arrange the trout on individual plates, divide the sauce among the trout, garnish with the lemon wedges, and serve immediately.

brown butter

Brown butter, with its pleasant and nutty flavor, is a classic accompaniment to simply cooked fish. With a few sage leaves, it can serve as a sauce for pasta or gnocchi.

To make brown butter, cook 6 tablespoons (¾ stick) unsalted butter in a skillet over moderate heat for 3 to 4 minutes, swirling the pan occasionally. The butter will melt, then foam slightly, and then begin to color. When the butter is a deep brown and has a toasty and nutty aroma, it's ready. Immediately add other cold or room-temperature ingredients, or pour the butter out of the pan to stop the cooking. Butter can go from brown to black and burned in a matter of moments.

chilean sea bass
with saffron sauce

Inspired by the flavors of the Provençal fish stew bouillabaisse, this dish is fragrant with saffron, garlic, tomato, and fennel. Saffron, the dried stigmas of the purple crocus flower, has the distinction of being the world's most expensive spice. Fortunately, a generous pinch is enough to flavor most recipes. It's available in thread or powder form; avoid the powdered variety, which loses its aroma quickly. Saffron can be found at most super-markets and gourmet stores and at bargain prices at Indian markets. Serve this dish with French bread, pasta, or risotto.

Serves 4

Season the fillets generously with salt and pepper. Set aside at room temperature for about 30 minutes. Combine the wine and saffron in a small bowl.

Heat a large, heavy sauté pan over high heat until very hot but not smoking. Add the oil and swirl to coat the bottom of the pan. Add the fillets, skinned side up, and cook without disturb-ing for 4 to 5 minutes, or until they release from the pan and are crusty and brown. Very gently, with a flexible fish spatula, turn the fillets over and continue to cook over high heat for another 3 to 4 minutes, or until they are just cooked through. The fillets will begin to flake at this point. Remove the fillets to a plate and tent with foil to keep warm.

Reduce the heat to medium; add the tomato, fennel, and garlic to the pan; and sauté for 1 to 2 minutes, or until the vegetables are soft. Add the saffron mixture and simmer for a minute or so, scraping up the browned bits from the bottom of the pan with a heatproof spatula. Add the broth and simmer for an-other 4 to 5 minutes, or until the sauce is thickened. Remove the pan from the heat and let cool for a minute or two. Whisk in the butter quickly, stir in the lemon juice and any accumu-lated juices from the fillets, and season with salt and pepper to taste.

Arrange the fillets on individual plates, divide the sauce among the fillets, and serve immediately.

Four 1-inch-thick Chilean sea bass fillets, weighing about 6 ounces each, skinned and boned

Kosher salt and freshly ground black pepper

¼ cup white wine

Generous pinch of saffron threads

3 tablespoons extra-virgin olive oil

1 Roma tomato, peeled, seeded, and diced

¼ cup diced fennel bulb

1 clove garlic, minced

½ cup fish or chicken broth

¼ cup (½ stick) cold unsalted butter, diced

1 teaspoon freshly squeezed lemon juice

vegetables, tofu, and fruit

"The prolonged contact with the hot pan allows the food to become a much deeper brown and to caramelize more."

For searing vegetables and fruits, the rules are the same as those for meat and fish. Start by selecting the freshest produce available. Fruit should be ripe but still firm or it will become mushy when cooked. Use a pan large enough to hold the ingredients in a single loose layer. Toss the food only after it browns and releases from the pan. If it seems to be browning too quickly, turn down the heat slightly, and add more oil to the pan anytime it looks dry. The food is done when it is fork-tender and nicely browned.

You may wonder how searing differs from sautéing when it comes to vegetables and fruits. In a sauté, the food is kept in motion throughout the cooking time. During searing, food is tossed much less frequently. The prolonged contact with the hot pan allows the food to become a much deeper brown and to caramelize more. However, because of their more irregular shape and smaller size, vegetables need to be turned more frequently than meat, poultry, or fish, so that more of the surface is exposed to the heat.

Searing tofu is a great way to enhance its texture. Use extra-firm tofu, which has a meatier texture and is therefore better for searing. For a nice brown crust, pat the tofu completely dry with paper towels immediately before adding it to the hot pan. Use a thin, flexible fish spatula to maneuver the tofu; even extra-firm tofu is too delicate to turn with tongs.

lemony seared asparagus

Select only thick asparagus stalks for this recipe, and be sure to use a pan large enough to fit them all in a single layer.

Serves 4

Heat a large, heavy sauté pan over medium-high heat until very hot but not smoking. Add 2 tablespoons of the oil and swirl to coat the bottom of the pan. Add the asparagus and cook for 5 to 6 minutes, tossing about 3 times, until tender-crisp and crusty and brown in spots, adding more of the oil as needed if the pan gets dry. Reduce the heat to medium-low, add the garlic and lemon zest (if using), and stir for a minute or so until fragrant.

Transfer the asparagus to a platter, drizzle with the lemon juice, season with salt and pepper to taste, and serve immediately.

2 to 3 tablespoons extra-virgin olive oil

1¼ pounds asparagus, trimmed of woody ends

1 clove garlic, minced

1 teaspoon grated lemon zest (optional)

1 to 2 teaspoons freshly squeezed lemon juice, to your taste

Kosher salt and freshly ground black pepper

green beans
with mint

Green beans must be cooked through until they are tender—undercooked or al dente green beans taste starchy and have an unpleasantly squeaky chew. As always, be sure to use a pan large enough to fit the beans in a single layer.   Serves 4

2 to 3 tablespoons extra-virgin olive oil

1 pound green beans, ends trimmed

1 clove garlic, minced

1 tablespoon minced fresh mint

Kosher salt and freshly ground black pepper

Heat a very large, heavy sauté pan over medium-high heat until very hot but not smoking. Add 2 tablespoons of the oil and swirl to coat the bottom of the pan. Add the green beans and cook for 10 to 12 minutes, tossing about 4 times, until tender and crusty and brown in spots, adding more of the oil as needed if the pan gets dry. Reduce the heat to medium-low, add the garlic, and stir for a minute or so until fragrant. Add the mint and season with salt and pepper to taste.

Transfer the green beans to a platter and serve immediately.

summer squash with basil

You can serve this as a side dish, toss the seared zucchini and yellow squash with cooked orzo, or stir them into risotto.

Serves 4

Heat a very large, heavy sauté pan over high heat until very hot but not smoking. Add the oil and swirl to coat the bottom of the pan. Add the zucchini and yellow squash and cook for 8 to 10 minutes, tossing about 4 times, until tender and crusty and brown in spots. Reduce the heat to medium-low, add the garlic, and stir for a minute or so until fragrant. Remove the pan from the heat and add the basil and Parmigiano-Reggiano cheese. Season with salt and pepper to taste.

Transfer the squash to a platter and serve immediately.

3 tablespoons extra-virgin olive oil

2 medium-size zucchini, diced

2 medium-size yellow squash, diced

2 cloves garlic, minced

6 to 8 leaves fresh basil, to your taste, torn

¼ cup freshly grated Parmigiano-Reggiano cheese

Kosher salt and freshly ground black pepper

garlicky broccoli with spaghetti

The idea of searing broccoli may be surprising, but it brings out an unexpected but satisfying richness and savory flavor from the vegetable. This dish can be put together in the time it takes for the pasta to cook; think of it as a speedy dinner solution after a busy day. Broccoli florets sear relatively quickly on each side and must be tossed periodically during cooking to expose more surfaces to the heat. The florets also tend to soak up the olive oil (and much of the oil vaporizes during searing), so it's important to add more oil while the broccoli cooks. Without an ample amount of oil, the broccoli won't cook evenly and will scorch. If you don't have a pan large enough to cook the entire amount of broccoli without overcrowding, sear it in two batches, using additional olive oil if the pan begins to look dry.

Serves 6 as a main course

1 pound spaghetti

1 to 1¼ cups extra-virgin olive oil

1½ pounds broccoli florets

6 cloves garlic, minced

Generous pinch of red pepper flakes, or to taste

Kosher salt and freshly ground black pepper

Freshly grated Parmigiano-Reggiano cheese for serving

In a large pot of boiling salted water, cook the spaghetti according to the package directions.

Meanwhile, heat a very large, heavy sauté pan over medium-high heat until very hot but not smoking. Add ¼ cup of the oil and swirl to coat the bottom of the pan. Add the broccoli and cook for 10 to 12 minutes, tossing 6 or 7 times, until tender and crusty and brown in spots. If the pan looks dry at any point, add more oil, about a tablespoon at a time—you may have to add oil as many as 5 or 6 times. Reduce the heat to medium-low and add the remaining ½ cup oil. Add the garlic and red pepper flakes and stir for a minute or so until fragrant. Season with salt and pepper to taste.

Drain the spaghetti when it is al dente. Add the spaghetti to the broccoli and toss to coat.

Arrange on individual plates, top with plenty of Parmigiano-Reggiano cheese, and serve immediately.

butternut squash with penne, italian sausage, and sage

An abundance of butternut squash in our garden inspired me to create this dish. I serve it at every fall gathering, from casual get-togethers to over-the-top wine dinners. Although any type of winter squash will work, butternut is the easiest to peel. The squash and the sausage must be seared separately so they each achieve a deep brown crust to create layers of complex and savory flavor in the finished dish.

Serves 6 as a main course

Heat a very large, heavy sauté pan over medium-high heat until very hot but not smoking. Add 4 tablespoons of the oil and swirl to coat the bottom of the pan. Add the squash and cook for 14 to 16 minutes, tossing about 3 times, until nearly tender and crusty and brown in spots. Remove the squash to a plate and tent with foil to keep warm.

Add the remaining 2 tablespoons oil to the pan and swirl to coat the bottom of the pan. Add the sausage and cook for 6 to 7 minutes, tossing about 2 times, until nearly cooked through and crusty and brown in spots. Reduce the heat to medium, add the garlic and red pepper flakes, and stir for a minute or so until fragrant. Add the wine and simmer for a minute or so, scraping up the browned bits from the bottom of the pan with a heatproof spatula. Return the squash to the pan, add the broth and sage, and simmer for 10 to 12 minutes, or until the sauce is thickened.

Meanwhile, in a large pot of boiling salted water, cook the penne according to the package directions. Drain when the pasta is al dente. Add the penne to the squash mixture and toss to coat. Season with salt and pepper to taste.

Arrange the pasta on individual plates, top with plenty of Parmigiano-Reggiano cheese, and serve immediately.

6 tablespoons extra-virgin olive oil

1 medium-size butternut squash, peeled, seeded, and cut into ¾-inch cubes

1½ pounds bulk Italian sausage, casings removed, crumbled

6 cloves garlic, minced

Generous pinch of red pepper flakes, or to taste

¼ cup white wine

1 cup chicken broth

3 tablespoons minced fresh sage

1 pound penne

Kosher salt and freshly ground black pepper

Freshly grated Parmigiano-Reggiano cheese for serving

sliced acorn squash

Here's a simple way to prepare squash that yields similar results to roasting but in a fraction of the time.

Serves 4

1 acorn squash, cut into
¾-inch-thick slices and
seeded

Kosher salt and freshly ground
black pepper

3 tablespoons extra-virgin
olive oil

Season the squash generously with salt and pepper. Heat a very large, heavy sauté pan over medium-high heat until very hot but not smoking. Add the oil and swirl to coat the bottom of the pan. Add the squash and cook without disturbing for 7 to 8 minutes, or until it releases from the pan and is crusty and brown. Using tongs, turn the squash over, reduce the heat to medium-low, and cook, covered, for another 6 to 7 minutes, or until tender.

Transfer the squash to a platter and serve immediately.

olive oil fries

These are the crunchiest and most delicious fries you can make without a deep fryer. Serve with ketchup or a flavored mayonnaise, if you wish.

Serves 4

Heat a very large, heavy sauté pan over medium-high heat until very hot but not smoking. Add the oil and swirl to coat the bottom of the pan. Add the potatoes and cook for 16 to 20 minutes, tossing 5 or 6 times, until tender and crusty and brown in spots. Season with salt and pepper to taste.

Transfer the potatoes to a platter and serve immediately.

3 tablespoons extra-virgin olive oil

4 small russet potatoes, peeled and cut into 3½ × ⅓ × ⅓-inch sticks

Kosher salt and freshly ground black pepper

eggplant with fresh mozzarella and tomato sauce

Here's a speedier and lighter version of the ever-popular eggplant Parmesan.   Serves 4

1 large eggplant, cut into 1-inch-thick slices

Kosher salt and freshly ground black pepper

6 tablespoons extra-virgin olive oil

8 ounces fresh mozzarella cheese, drained and sliced, at room temperature

2 cloves garlic, minced

One 14½-ounce can diced tomatoes, drained

6 to 8 leaves fresh basil, to your taste, torn

3 tablespoons freshly grated Parmigiano-Reggiano cheese

Season the eggplant generously with salt and pepper. Heat a very large, heavy sauté pan over medium-high heat until very hot but not smoking. Add 3 tablespoons of the oil and swirl to coat the bottom of the pan. Add the eggplant and cook without disturbing for 3 to 4 minutes, or until it releases from the pan and is crusty and brown. Using tongs, turn the eggplant over, add another 2 tablespoons oil, and continue to cook over medium-high heat for another 3 to 4 minutes, or until tender. Remove the eggplant to a plate, quickly top each slice of eggplant with a slice or two of mozzarella, and tent with foil to melt the cheese and keep warm.

Reduce the heat to medium, add the remaining 1 tablespoon oil and the garlic to the pan, and sauté for 30 seconds, or until fragrant. Add the tomatoes and simmer, scraping up the browned bits from the bottom of the pan with a heatproof spatula, for 1 to 2 minutes, or until the sauce is thickened. Stir in the basil and season with salt and pepper to taste.

Arrange the mozzarella-topped eggplant on individual plates, divide the sauce among the eggplant, sprinkle with the Parmigiano-Reggiano cheese, and serve immediately.

marinated
portobello mushrooms

Portobello mushrooms have such a meaty texture that they can be cooked and served
just like steak. Serves 4

Combine the soy sauce, honey, sesame oil, garlic, and a generous pinch of pepper in a large zipper-top plastic bag. Add the
mushrooms and turn to coat. Seal the bag, letting out all the
air. Marinate the mushrooms for about 30 minutes.

Remove the mushrooms from the marinade and pat dry with
paper towels; discard the marinade. Heat a large, heavy sauté
pan over medium-high heat until very hot but not smoking.
Add the oil and swirl to coat the bottom of the pan. Add the
mushrooms, gill side up, and cook without disturbing for 2 to
3 minutes, or until they release from the pan and are crusty and
brown. Using tongs, turn the mushrooms over and continue
to cook over medium-high heat for another 1 to 2 minutes, or
until tender.

Transfer the mushrooms to a platter and serve immediately.

2 tablespoons soy sauce

1 tablespoon honey

1 teaspoon dark sesame oil

2 cloves garlic, minced

Freshly ground black pepper

4 portobello mushrooms,
stemmed

3 tablespoons canola oil

seared
wild mushrooms

Any fresh wild mushrooms, alone or in combination, are delicious in this simple recipe. Chanterelles, hedgehogs, oysters, lobsters, and porcinis are all available in the fall, and morels are plentiful in the springtime. To prepare the mushrooms, trim the ends with a paring knife and brush them clean with a dry pastry brush. Use water to clean only the most stubborn dirt. Cut lobster, porcini, or morel mushrooms into bite-size pieces with a knife. Use your fingers to tear large chanterelles, hedgehogs, or oysters into smaller pieces to preserve their natural shapes. Mushrooms are mostly water, and they will exude liquid if they are cooked over low heat or if the pan is overcrowded. Most cooks have probably experienced this problem at some point and tasted the slimy, soggy results. So practicing good searing technique is especially important when cooking mushrooms. The mushrooms will cook up golden brown, and the high heat will concentrate their savory flavor and enhance their meaty texture. Serve the mushrooms as a side dish with steak or duck breasts, or use them as a topping for salad, pasta, risotto, or polenta.

Serves 4

3 to 6 tablespoons extra-virgin olive oil

1 pound wild mushrooms, sliced or torn into bite-size pieces

1 teaspoon minced fresh thyme

1 shallot, minced

Kosher salt and freshly ground black pepper

Heat a very large, heavy sauté pan over high heat until very hot but not smoking. Add 3 tablespoons of the oil and swirl to coat the bottom of the pan. Add the mushrooms to the pan and cook for 6 to 7 minutes, tossing about 4 times, until tender and crusty and brown in spots. If the pan looks dry at any point, add more oil, about a tablespoon at a time—you may have to add oil as many as 2 or 3 times. Reduce the heat to medium-low, add the thyme and shallot, and stir for a minute or so until fragrant. Season with salt and pepper to taste.

Transfer the mushrooms to a platter and serve immediately.

brussels sprouts with caramelized onions

Brussels sprouts become sweet when seared, so they go well with caramelized onions.

Serves 4

Heat a large, heavy sauté pan over medium-high heat until very hot but not smoking. Add the oil and swirl to coat the bottom of the pan. Add the Brussels sprouts and cook for 7 to 8 minutes, tossing about 4 times, until tender and crusty and brown in spots. Add the caramelized onions and season with salt and pepper to taste.

Transfer the sprouts to a platter and serve immediately.

¼ cup extra-virgin olive oil

16 Brussels sprouts, trimmed and quartered

½ cup caramelized onions (page 21)

Kosher salt and freshly ground black pepper

cauliflower with capers and parsley

Most cooks steam, simmer, or boil cauliflower, but this vegetable is a great candidate for searing. Deeply browned cauliflower is rich, satisfying, and almost meaty. Keep in mind that cauliflower should be cooked until tender throughout—the term tender-crisp does not apply to this vegetable.

Serves 4

¼ to ½ cup extra-virgin olive oil

1 pound cauliflower florets

1 shallot, minced

2 cloves garlic, minced

2 anchovy fillets, minced

2 tablespoons capers

1 tablespoon minced Italian parsley

1 teaspoon freshly squeezed lemon juice

Kosher salt and freshly ground black pepper

Heat a large, heavy sauté pan over medium heat until very hot but not smoking. Add ¼ cup of the oil and swirl to coat the bottom of the pan. Add the cauliflower and cook for 14 to 16 minutes, tossing 6 or 7 times, until tender and crusty and brown in spots. If the pan looks dry at any point, add more oil, about a tablespoon at a time—you may have to add oil as many as 3 or 4 times. Reduce the heat to medium-low; add the shallot, garlic, and anchovies; and stir for a minute or so until fragrant. Stir in the capers, parsley, and lemon juice and season with salt and pepper to taste.

Transfer the cauliflower to a platter and serve immediately.

cauliflower with indian flavors

Cauliflower goes especially well with ginger and other Indian flavors. For a vegetarian meal, serve this dish with Spiced Basmati Rice (page 137).   Serves 4

Heat a large, heavy sauté pan over medium heat until very hot but not smoking. Add ¼ cup of the oil and swirl to coat the bottom of the pan. Add the cauliflower and cook for 14 to 16 minutes, tossing 6 or 7 times, until tender and crusty and brown in spots. If the pan looks dry at any point, add more oil, about a tablespoon at a time—you may have to add oil as many as 3 or 4 times. Reduce the heat to medium-low; add the ginger, garlic, and curry powder; and stir for a minute or so until fragrant. Add the cilantro and season with salt to taste.

Transfer the cauliflower to a platter and serve immediately.

¼ to ½ cup canola oil

1 pound cauliflower florets

1 tablespoon minced fresh ginger

2 cloves garlic, minced

1 teaspoon curry powder

2 tablespoons minced fresh cilantro

Kosher salt

tofu with vegetables and peanut sauce

Firm tofu has a great texture for searing, but because of its mild flavor, it must be marinated or served with a lively sauce. It's important to pat the tofu until it is as dry as possible so that excess moisture doesn't prevent it from browning. If you are not familiar with the technique of julienne, see the tutorial on my blog, Hungry Cravings (http://hungrycravings.com). Be sure to buy coconut milk, not cream of coconut, and shake the can before using. Jasmine rice is the perfect accompaniment to this dish.

Serves 4

One 14-ounce package extra-firm tofu, cut into four 1-inch-thick slices

Kosher salt and freshly ground black pepper

2 tablespoons canola oil

1 cup broccoli florets

1 cup julienned red bell pepper

½ cup julienned carrot

1 cup julienned snow peas

1 cup bean sprouts

3 cloves garlic, minced

1 tablespoon minced fresh ginger

1 red Thai chile, seeded and minced

1 teaspoon curry powder

One 14-ounce can coconut milk

⅓ cup creamy peanut butter

Gently pat the tofu slices dry with paper towels. Season them generously with salt and pepper and set aside at room temperature for about 30 minutes.

Heat a large, heavy sauté pan over medium-high heat until very hot but not smoking. Add the canola oil and swirl to coat the bottom of the pan. Add the tofu and cook without disturbing for 3 to 4 minutes, or until it releases from the pan and is crusty and brown. Very gently, with a flexible fish spatula, turn the tofu over and continue to cook over medium-high heat for another 2 to 3 minutes, or until it is heated through. Remove the tofu to a plate and tent with foil to keep warm.

Add the broccoli to the pan and stir-fry for a minute or so. Add the bell pepper and carrot and stir-fry for a minute more. Add the snow peas and bean sprouts and stir-fry for another minute, or until the vegetables are tender-crisp. Remove the vegetables to a plate and tent with foil to keep warm.

Reduce the heat to medium; add the garlic, ginger, chile, and curry powder to the pan; and sauté for 30 seconds, or until fragrant. Add the coconut milk, peanut butter, soy sauce, and brown sugar and simmer, whisking to dissolve the peanut butter, for 1 to 2 minutes, or until the sauce is thickened. Remove the pan from the heat and stir in the cilantro, lime juice, and sesame oil.

Spoon some of the sauce into the center of each of four plates. Arrange a slice of tofu atop each pool of sauce, top with the vegetables, and sprinkle with the peanuts and green onions. Serve immediately.

2 tablespoons soy sauce

1 tablespoon light brown sugar

2 tablespoons minced fresh cilantro

1 tablespoon freshly squeezed lime juice

Several drops of dark sesame oil, to your taste

2 tablespoons crushed roasted peanuts

2 tablespoons sliced green onions

tofu with mushroom gravy

A combination of white button, oyster, and shiitake mushrooms works best in this dish. You can find Shaoxing rice wine in Asian markets, or you can substitute sherry or sake.

Serves 4

2 tablespoons Shaoxing rice wine

2 tablespoons soy sauce

2 cloves garlic, minced

One 14-ounce package extra-firm tofu, cut into four 1-inch-thick slices

1 tablespoon cornstarch

1 tablespoon water

3 tablespoons canola oil

8 ounces mushrooms, sliced

1½ cups vegetable broth

Freshly ground black pepper

Combine the rice wine, soy sauce, and garlic in a large zipper-top plastic bag. Add the tofu and turn to coat. Seal the bag, letting out all the air. Marinate the tofu for about 30 minutes at room temperature. Whisk together the cornstarch and water in a small bowl.

Remove the tofu from the marinade, reserving the marinade, and gently pat the tofu dry with paper towels. Heat a large, heavy sauté pan over medium-high heat until very hot but not smoking. Add the oil and swirl to coat the bottom of the pan. Add the tofu and cook without disturbing for 3 to 4 minutes, or until it releases from the pan and is crusty and brown. Very gently, with a flexible fish spatula, turn the tofu over and continue to cook over medium-high heat for another 2 to 3 minutes, or until it is heated through. Remove the tofu to a plate and tent with foil to keep warm.

Add the mushrooms to the pan and sauté for 3 to 4 minutes, or until soft. Add the reserved marinade and simmer for a minute or so, scraping up the browned bits from the bottom of the pan with a heatproof spatula. Add the broth and bring to a boil. Stir the cornstarch mixture to recombine and whisk it into the gravy. Simmer for another minute, or until the gravy is thickened. Season with pepper to taste.

Arrange the tofu on individual plates, divide the gravy among the tofu slices, and serve immediately.

seared pear and blue cheese salad

Serve this salad in the fall, when pears are in season. Choose any variety of ripe but firm pears, so that they will retain their texture once they are cooked. Walnut oil adds a rich, nutty flavor to the dish. Store the oil in the refrigerator, as it can go rancid quickly. You can substitute an extra tablespoon of olive oil for the walnut oil.

Serves 4

Whisk together the vinegar, honey, and shallot in a medium-size bowl. Continue whisking while adding the walnut oil and 2 tablespoons of the olive oil in a thin stream. Season with salt and pepper to taste.

Heat a large, heavy sauté pan over high heat until very hot but not smoking. Add the remaining 2 tablespoons olive oil and swirl to coat the bottom of the pan. Add the pears and cook for 6 to 7 minutes, tossing about 3 times, until tender and crusty and brown in spots. Combine the greens and vinaigrette in a large bowl and toss to coat.

Mound a portion of the greens in the center of each plate and sprinkle with the blue cheese, cranberries, and walnuts. Divide the pears among the plates and serve immediately.

2 tablespoons cider vinegar

1 tablespoon honey

1 shallot, minced

1 tablespoon walnut oil

¼ cup extra-virgin olive oil

Kosher salt and freshly ground black pepper

3 firm ripe pears, peeled, cored, and cut into sixths

5 ounces mesclun greens

1¼ cups crumbled blue cheese

¼ cup dried cranberries

¼ cup walnut pieces, toasted

mango and brie on baguette

Select mangoes that just yield to gentle pressure for this recipe. Very ripe mangoes are too juicy and soft for searing. Mangoes can be a bit slippery, but they're easy to work with once you get the hang of it. Each mango has a large, thick seed that runs its length. Peel the fruit with either a paring knife or a vegetable peeler, and then use a knife to cut the fleshy cheeks off either side of the seed. These mango cheeks are ideal for searing. You can trim the remaining flesh from the pit and reserve it for another use, such as Firecracker Chicken Breasts with Mango Sauce (page 64) or Chile-Rubbed Salmon with Mango Salsa (page 88); or do as I do and just nibble on it when no one else is looking. Rather than cutting the baguette into four pieces and assembling individual sandwiches, I find that it's much easier and more efficient to build one long sandwich and then cut it. This also results in a pretty presentation, with all of the layers of the filling neatly exposed. Use a serrated bread knife to split the baguette lengthwise and again to cut individual sandwich portions.

Serves 4

12 ounces Brie cheese, sliced

1 baguette, split lengthwise

¼ cup extra-virgin olive oil

3 large mangoes, peeled and seeds removed

4 ounces baby arugula

Kosher salt

Arrange the sliced Brie on the bottom half of the baguette. Heat a heavy sauté pan over high heat until very hot but not smoking. Add 3 tablespoons of the oil and swirl to coat the bottom of the pan. Add the mangoes, cut side down, and cook without disturbing for 2 to 3 minutes, or until they release from the pan and are crusty and brown. Very gently, with a flexible fish spatula, turn the mangoes over and continue to cook over high heat for another 1 to 2 minutes, or until they are tender.

Arrange the mangoes on the Brie, top with the arugula, drizzle with the remaining 1 tablespoon oil, and season with salt to taste. Cover with the top half of the baguette and cut into eighths.

Arrange the sandwiches on individual plates and serve immediately.

seared nectarines
with raspberry sorbet

Select ripe but firm nectarines for searing. Peaches can be substituted.   Serves 4

Heat a large, heavy sauté pan over high heat until very hot but not smoking. Add the oil and swirl to coat the bottom of the pan. Add the nectarine halves, cut side down, and cook without disturbing for 2 to 3 minutes, or until they release from the pan and are crusty and brown.

Arrange the nectarine halves, cut side up, on individual plates, top each with a scoop of the sorbet, garnish with the mint, and serve immediately.

3 tablespoons canola oil

2 large nectarines, halved and pitted

1 pint raspberry sorbet

4 sprigs fresh mint, for garnish

pineapple with vanilla ice cream and coconut-caramel sauce

Pineapple, with its firm and fibrous flesh, is the perfect fruit for searing. It is the base for this tropical sundae, in which coconut milk is used instead of heavy cream in the caramel sauce. (Do not use cream of coconut.) Use a 1-inch round cookie cutter to core the pineapple slices.

Serves 6

One 14-ounce can coconut milk

1 cup sugar

¼ cup water

3 tablespoons canola oil

1 pineapple, peeled, cut into 1-inch-thick slices, and cored

3 cups vanilla ice cream

¼ cup shredded unsweetened coconut, toasted

Simmer the coconut milk in a small, heavy saucepan for 16 to 20 minutes, or until reduced by about half.

Meanwhile, combine the sugar and water in another small, heavy saucepan, and bring to a boil. Using a pastry brush dipped in water, wash down any errant sugar crystals from the sides of the pan, and boil for 6 to 7 minutes, or until the sugar is fragrant and a deep amber color. Prepare an ice-water bath. Remove the pan from the heat and dip the bottom into the ice-water bath for a second or two. Slowly stir in the coconut milk. Set the pan over low heat and stir until smooth.

Heat a very large, heavy sauté pan over high heat until very hot but not smoking. Add the oil and swirl to coat the bottom of the pan. Add the pineapple and cook without disturbing for 3 to 4 minutes, or until it releases from the pan and is crusty and brown. Using tongs, turn the pineapple over and continue to cook over high heat for another 1 to 2 minutes, or until tender.

Arrange the pineapple slices on individual plates. Top each with a scoop of the ice cream, drizzle with some of the sauce, sprinkle with shredded coconut, and serve immediately.

caramelized apples

Cooking Golden Delicious apples brings out their floral and buttery flavors. These apples are a fantastic addition to both sweet and savory dishes—tossed in a fall salad, stirred into squash soup, spooned over pork chops, or as a topping for vanilla ice cream.   Serves 4

Heat a large, heavy sauté pan over medium-high heat until very hot but not smoking. Add the butter and swirl to coat the bottom of the pan. Add the apples and cook for 6 to 7 minutes, tossing about 2 times, until tender and crusty and brown in spots. Remove the pan from the heat and stir in the sugar and cinnamon.

Transfer the apples to a bowl and serve immediately.

3 tablespoons unsalted butter, diced

2 Golden Delicious apples, peeled, cored, and diced

1 tablespoon light brown sugar

⅛ teaspoon ground cinnamon

caramel sauce

Caramel sauce is easy to make, but a few precautions are necessary to avoid burns and crystallizing the sugar. Use a small, heavy saucepan and heatproof utensils with wooden handles—metal utensils conduct heat and can become too hot to handle. The saucepan, all of the utensils, and the sugar must be very clean, as impurities can cause the sugar to crystallize. Add the sugar to the pan and just enough water to moisten it. Bring the mixture to a rolling boil to dissolve all of the sugar. At this point, wash down the sides of the pan with a pastry brush dipped in water to eliminate any errant sugar crystals. Continue to cook the sugar syrup at a rolling boil. After several minutes, the sugar will begin to color around the edges of the pan. You can swirl the pan gently, but do not stir; too much agitation can cause crystallization. The sugar is ready when it is a deep amber color, or a candy thermometer registers about 335°F.

Keep in mind that caramel can go from perfect to burned in a matter of seconds. So when it is done, you must be ready to stop the cooking immediately. Dip the bottom of the saucepan into an ice-water bath for a moment. Have ready some warm heavy cream, or, in the case of the Coconut-Caramel Sauce, reduced coconut milk, and stir it in slowly and carefully. It will boil up and spit and spatter. Never use cold cream because it will cause the caramel sauce to boil up furiously and may even cause crystallization. Continue to add enough cream to reach the desired consistency. The caramel sauce should be gooey but not chewy when it cools. Vanilla may also be added at this point. Set the pan over low heat and stir until smooth. Serve the caramel sauce warm.

caramelized banana sundaes

Bananas that are just ripe and still firm are best for searing. Avoid very ripe bananas, which will turn to mush. If you are a chocoholic, use chocolate ice cream instead of vanilla.

Serves 4

¼ cup heavy cream

2 ounces semisweet chocolate chips

1 tablespoon banana liqueur

2 tablespoons unsalted butter, diced

2 bananas, peeled and cut into ¾-inch-thick slices

½ teaspoon ground cinnamon

Generous pinch of freshly grated nutmeg

2 cups vanilla ice cream

¼ cup pecan pieces, toasted

In a small, heavy saucepan, bring the cream to a simmer. Place the chocolate chips in a medium-size bowl and add the hot cream and liqueur. Whisk until smooth.

Heat a very large, heavy sauté pan over medium-high heat until very hot but not smoking. Add the butter and swirl to coat the bottom of the pan. Add the bananas and cook without disturbing for 2 to 3 minutes, or until they release from the pan and are crusty and brown. Using a spatula, turn the bananas over and continue to cook over medium-high heat for another 1 to 2 minutes, or until tender. Remove the pan from the heat and stir in the cinnamon and nutmeg.

Place a scoop of the ice cream in each of four bowls, divide the bananas among them, drizzle with the chocolate sauce, and sprinkle with the pecans. Serve immediately.

side dishes

"Not everything can be seared. And who wants to eat a meal in which every dish has the same texture?"

Not everything can be seared. And who wants to eat a meal in which every dish has the same texture? Sometimes a baked potato, steamed rice, pasta tossed with olive oil, buttered seasonal vegetables, or a green salad is called for. Here's a variety of other side dishes that pair well with the seared entrée recipes in this book.

potato gratin

Use thinly sliced Yukon Gold potatoes, which become creamy but retain their texture after cooking. A mandoline makes easy work of slicing potatoes, but it can also be done with a chef's knife. Season the gratin carefully before it goes into the oven. I toss the potato slices with salt and pepper in a large bowl and taste a small bit of raw potato to check the amount of salt—it should taste slightly salty at this point for a perfect finished gratin—and spit it out. If your baking dish is a different size or shape from the one recommended here, use it, but keep in mind that you may have to adjust the amount of cream. As long as you add enough cream to just reach the bottom of the top layer of potatoes, the gratin will turn out great. Letting the gratin rest before serving makes it possible to cut neat portions. The simple potato gratin, delicious as is, can be embellished by varying the type of cheese or adding a filling. Try grated Parmigiano-Reggiano or crumbled blue cheese instead of the Gruyère. Chopped cooked spinach (or thawed frozen spinach that has been squeezed dry), sautéed leek slices, caramelized onions (page 21), or sautéed mushrooms are all good filling choices. Arrange approximately half of the potatoes in the gratin dish, layer in about a cup of the ingredient of your choice, arrange the remaining potatoes, and top with the cheese. Serve the gratin with almost any dish in this book. It goes particularly well with beef, lamb, and duck. Serves 6

Preheat the oven to 325°F. Generously butter a 12-inch oval baking dish. Season the potato slices with salt and pepper to taste. Layer them into the dish, arranging them in neat overlapping ovals. Stir the garlic and nutmeg into the cream and slowly pour the mixture over the potatoes. Sprinkle evenly with the Gruyère cheese. Bake for 1 to 1¼ hours, or until the top is golden brown and the potatoes are tender. Cover with foil to keep warm and allow to rest for 20 to 25 minutes.

Cut into portions and serve immediately.

Unsalted butter, for greasing the baking dish

6 large Yukon Gold potatoes (about 3 pounds), peeled and cut into ⅛-inch-thick slices

Kosher salt and freshly ground black pepper

1 clove garlic, grated

Generous pinch of freshly grated nutmeg

1¾ cups heavy cream

1 cup shredded Gruyère cheese

truffled mashed potatoes

Put a gourmet spin on the classic "meat and potatoes" with this luxurious but simple recipe. Cooking the potatoes whole and pureeing them with a food mill or ricer yields the lightest, fluffiest, silky-smooth texture imaginable. There's no need to peel the potatoes; the mill or ricer will hold back the skins. If you prefer chunky, home-style potatoes, peel them and use a potato masher instead. Although fresh truffles are prohibitively expensive, truffle oil is quite affordable. A little bit goes a long way, and a mere drizzle is enough to flavor any dish. Look for it at gourmet markets or specialty stores. Truffle oil keeps for months stored in the refrigerator. Chilled, it becomes cloudy and solidifies, so let it come to room temperature for about 15 minutes before using. You can pair this dish with most of the entrées in this book, especially those that feature beef tenderloin or mushrooms.

Serves 4 to 6

3 medium-size russet potatoes (about 2 pounds)

Kosher salt

¾ cup heavy cream

½ cup (1 stick) unsalted butter, melted

1 teaspoon truffle oil

Freshly ground black pepper

Place the potatoes in a medium-size saucepan and add enough water to cover by several inches. Add several large pinches of salt. Bring to a boil and simmer for 30 to 35 minutes, or until tender. In a small, heavy saucepan, bring the cream to a simmer. Drain the potatoes and process them with a food mill or ricer into a large bowl. Stir in the cream, butter, and truffle oil. Season with salt and pepper to taste.

Transfer the potatoes to a bowl and serve immediately.

baked
sweet potatoes

If you eat sweet potatoes only in a casserole loaded with cinnamon, brown sugar, and marshmallows at Thanksgiving time, you're missing out. Their sweet and earthy flavor is best appreciated with nothing more than a pat of butter. I've served these to family and friends, and they're always so surprised and delighted. Orange-fleshed sweet potatoes cook up moist and creamy and are my favorite; yellow ones turn out fluffy, like russets. This dish is a nice change from regular baked potatoes, and it goes particularly well with spicy foods. Serve it alongside any of the chile-laden recipes in this book, such as Chile-Lime Marinated Rib-Eye Steaks (page 22), Steaks with Chipotle Cream Sauce (page 24), or Buffalo Quail with Southwestern Ranch Dressing (page 73).   Serves 4

Preheat the oven to 350°F. Arrange the sweet potatoes on a foil-lined baking sheet and bake for 1 to 1¼ hours, or until tender.

Cut a slit in the top of each sweet potato and squeeze open. Top each with 1 tablespoon of the butter and season with pepper to taste. Serve immediately.

4 large sweet potatoes, weighing about 1 pound each

¼ cup (½ stick) salted butter, softened

Freshly ground black pepper

quinoa pilaf

Quinoa is a super-healthful grain with a mildly nutty flavor and pleasant texture. It's quick and easy to prepare, and you can tell it's cooked through when it becomes tender and translucent and the curlicue-shaped germ is visible. Quinoa is a nice alternative to the usual rice or potatoes and goes well with any entrée in this book, especially the pork, chicken, and fish dishes. Try it with Smoky Chicken Breasts with Sherry Sauce (page 62) or Salmon Fillets with Green Peppercorn Sauce (page 89).   Serves 6

3 tablespoons unsalted butter

½ medium-size yellow onion, diced

1 celery stalk, diced

1 carrot, diced

2 cloves garlic, minced

1 teaspoon minced fresh thyme

1½ cups quinoa

2½ cups chicken broth or water

1 bay leaf

Kosher salt and freshly ground black pepper

1 tablespoon minced Italian parsley

Heat a medium-size, heavy saucepan over medium heat. Add the butter, onion, celery, and carrot and sauté for 5 to 6 minutes, or until soft. Add the garlic and thyme and sauté for another 1 to 2 minutes, or until fragrant. Add the quinoa and stir until coated with the butter. Add the broth and bay leaf, season with salt and pepper to taste, and bring to a boil. Cover, reduce the heat to low, and cook for 20 to 22 minutes, or until the quinoa is tender and all of the liquid has been absorbed. Discard the bay leaf, stir in the parsley, and fluff with a fork.

Transfer the quinoa to a bowl and serve immediately.

spiced basmati rice

Look for brown cardamom and imported basmati rice, which is much more aromatic than domestically grown rice, at Indian markets. Serve this fragrant rice dish as an accompaniment to any Indian-inspired main course.

Serves 4

Melt the butter in a small, heavy saucepan over medium heat. Add the cinnamon, cloves, peppercorns, cardamom, and cumin seeds and toast, stirring constantly, for 1 to 2 minutes, or until fragrant. Add the rice and stir until coated with the butter. Add the water and season with salt to taste, bring to a boil, and boil for 3 to 4 minutes, or until the water is reduced so that it comes just below the top of the rice and craters form on the surface. Cover, reduce the heat to low, and cook without disturbing for 18 to 20 minutes, or until the rice is tender and all of the liquid has been absorbed. Remove from the heat and allow to rest for 10 to 12 minutes.

Fluff the rice with a fork. Transfer the rice to a platter and serve immediately.

3 tablespoons unsalted butter

1 cinnamon stick

2 whole cloves

5 black peppercorns

2 brown cardamom pods, crushed

¼ teaspoon cumin seeds

1 cup basmati rice

1½ cups water

Kosher salt

rice noodle salad

This Vietnamese-inspired recipe makes a lot, but you will want leftovers. Rice vermicelli, fish sauce, Thai chiles, and black sesame seeds can be found at Asian markets and gourmet grocers. If you are not familiar with the technique of julienne, see the tutorial on my blog, Hungry Cravings (http://hungrycravings.com). The salad goes well with any of the Asian-flavored entrées in this book, particularly the fish dishes.   Serves 6 to 8

6¾ ounces rice vermicelli

¼ cup fish sauce

¼ cup freshly squeezed lime juice

¼ cup light brown sugar

2 cloves garlic, minced

1 red Thai chile, seeded and minced

2 cups shredded napa cabbage

1 cup julienned carrot

1 cup julienned English cucumber

1 cup julienned red bell pepper

1 cup julienned snow peas

1 cup bean sprouts

½ cup minced fresh cilantro

½ cup sliced green onions

2 tablespoons black sesame seeds

Place the vermicelli in a medium-size bowl, add enough boiling water to cover by several inches, and let soak for 10 to 12 minutes, or until rehydrated and tender. Drain well and let cool.

To make the dressing, combine the fish sauce, lime juice, brown sugar, garlic, and chile in a small bowl. In a large bowl, combine the cabbage, carrot, cucumber, bell pepper, snow peas, bean sprouts, cilantro, green onions, sesame seeds, and rice noodles. Add the dressing and toss to coat.

Transfer the salad to a platter and serve immediately.

creamed spinach

Fresh spinach requires tedious preparation—washing, stemming, chopping, blanching, and shocking in cold water—so I take a shortcut and use frozen spinach, and the results are just as good. It's important to squeeze all of the liquid from the thawed frozen spinach, or the dish will be soupy. The recipe can be prepared up to a day in advance, covered, and refrigerated; bake it right before serving. This steak house classic is the perfect side dish for steaks, chops, or duck breasts.

Serves 6

Preheat the oven to 375°F. Generously butter a 9-inch oval baking dish. Heat a medium-size, heavy sauté pan over medium-low heat. Add the butter and onion and sauté for 5 to 6 minutes, or until soft. Add the garlic and sauté for another 1 to 2 minutes, or until fragrant. Remove from the heat; stir in the spinach, cream, and nutmeg; and season with salt and pepper to taste.

Transfer the mixture to the baking dish and sprinkle evenly with the Parmigiano-Reggiano cheese. Bake for 30 to 35 minutes, or until the mixture is bubbling around the edges and the top is golden brown. Serve immediately.

1½ tablespoons unsalted butter, plus more for greasing the baking dish

½ medium-size yellow onion, diced

2 cloves garlic, minced

Two 10-ounce packages frozen chopped spinach, thawed and squeezed dry

1½ cups heavy cream

Generous pinch of freshly grated nutmeg

Kosher salt and freshly ground black pepper

⅓ cup freshly grated Parmigiano-Reggiano cheese

braised
swiss chard

Before cooking, wash the chard and shake it dry, leaving just enough water still clinging to the leaves to facilitate the braising. The stems and ribs must cook longer than the
leaves since they are much more substantial; they add a nice crunch to the dish. All of
the chard may not fit into the pan at first; add as much as possible, and then add more
as the leaves wilt down. The recipe calls for starting the garlic in a cold pan, which infuses
the dish with a sweet and mellow garlicky flavor. Accompany any lamb or duck entrées
with this dish.

Serves 4

3 tablespoons extra-virgin
olive oil

2 to 3 cloves garlic, to your
taste, thinly sliced

Generous pinch of red pepper
flakes, or to taste

2 bunches Swiss chard (about
1 pound), stems and ribs
diced and leaves cut into
1-inch-wide strips

1 teaspoon freshly squeezed
lemon juice

Kosher salt and freshly ground
black pepper

Combine the oil and garlic in a large, heavy sauté pan and heat
over medium heat. Sauté the garlic for 3 to 4 minutes, or until
golden brown. Add the red pepper flakes and chard stems and
ribs and sauté for another 2 to 3 minutes, or until the chard
is slightly softened. Add the chard leaves and sauté for 2 to
3 minutes more, or until they are just wilted. Cover, reduce the
heat to medium-low, and cook for 5 to 6 minutes, or until the
chard is tender. Stir in the lemon juice and season with salt and
pepper to taste.

Transfer the chard to a bowl and serve immediately.

steamed baby bok choy

Steamed baby bok choy is vibrantly green, and the juicy stems become tender and somehow creamy. You may omit the soy sauce or oyster sauce in favor of drizzling the bok choy with the sauce from your main course. Fragrant sesame oil is also a nice choice for adding flavor to steamed bok choy. Serve this alongside any soy sauce–based dish, including Rib-Eye Steaks with Soy-Butter Sauce (page 23), Hanger Steaks with Shiitake Sauce (page 26), or Tofu with Mushroom Gravy (page 124). **Serves 4**

In a medium-size, heavy saucepan, bring an inch of water to a simmer over medium-low heat. Place the bok choy in a steamer insert and set over the simmering water. Cover and steam for 6 to 7 minutes, or until bright green and tender.

Transfer the bok choy to a platter, drizzle with the soy sauce, sprinkle with the sesame seeds, and serve immediately.

3 heads baby bok choy, leaves separated

1 tablespoon soy sauce or oyster sauce

2 teaspoons sesame seeds, toasted

roasted tomatoes

Basil, mint, rosemary, or a combination of herbs can be used in place of the oregano in this dish. Serve these juicy tomatoes with any lamb dish. They also go well with Mediterranean-inspired recipes, such as Provençal Duck Breasts (page 70) or Halibut with Salsa Verde (page 92). Serves 4

1 pint cherry or grape tomatoes, halved

1 clove garlic, minced

1 teaspoon minced fresh oregano

2 tablespoons extra-virgin olive oil

Kosher salt and freshly ground black pepper

Preheat the oven to 450°F. Combine the tomatoes, garlic, oregano, and olive oil in a medium-size bowl and season with salt and pepper to taste. Arrange the tomatoes in a single layer on a foil-lined baking sheet and bake for 16 to 18 minutes, or until the tomatoes are tender and juicy.

Transfer the tomatoes to a bowl and serve immediately.

resources

dean & deluca

www.deandeluca.com

Specialty groceries, including ancho chile powder, black sesame seeds, five-spice powder, foie gras, garam masala, green peppercorns, herbes de Provence, Hungarian paprika, lavender, Mexican oregano, pasilla chile powder, salmon roe, Spanish paprika, and truffle oil.

jamba juice

www.jambajuice.com

Fresh carrot juice.

nicky usa

www.nickyusa.com

Meat and game, including duck breasts, foie gras, lamb, and semiboneless quail.

penzeys spices

www.penzeys.com

Herbs and spices, including black sesame seeds, brown cardamom, five-spice powder, *fleur de sel,* garam masala, green peppercorns, Hungarian paprika, kosher salt, lavender, Mexican oregano, saffron, Spanish paprika, and vanilla beans.

the spanish table

www.spanishtable.com

Spanish foods, including green peppercorns in brine, saffron, Spanish chorizo, and Spanish paprika.

sur la table

www.surlatable.com

Cooking tools and equipment, including All-Clad cookware, digital probe thermometers, fish spatulas, heatproof spatulas, splatter screens, and tongs.

the tao of tea

www.taooftea.com

Matcha.

whole foods market

www.wholefoodsmarket.com

High-quality groceries, including black sesame seeds, bonito flakes, Boursin, canned chipotles in adobo sauce, dried porcini mushrooms, dried shiitake mushrooms, duck breasts, fish sauce, five-spice powder, free-range and organic chicken, French green lentils, garam masala, Gorgonzola cheese, green peppercorns, green peppercorns in brine, herbes de Provence, imported basmati rice, kelp, kosher salt, lavender, natural beef, natural lamb, natural pork, organic produce, prosciutto, pure pressed carrot juice, quinoa, rice vermicelli, saffron, Spanish paprika, sustainable seafood, truffle oil, vanilla beans, and walnut oil.

williams-sonoma

www.williams-sonoma.com

Cooking tools and equipment, including All-Clad cookware, digital probe thermometers, fish spatulas, heatproof spatulas, splatter screens, and tongs.

measurement equivalents

Please note that all conversions are approximate.

liquid conversions

U.S.	Metric	U.S.	Metric
1 tsp	5 ml	1 cup	240 ml
1 tbs	15 ml	1 cup + 2 tbs	275 ml
2 tbs	30 ml	$1^1/_4$ cups	300 ml
3 tbs	45 ml	$1^1/_3$ cups	325 ml
$^1/_4$ cup	60 ml	$1^1/_2$ cups	350 ml
$^1/_3$ cup	75 ml	$1^2/_3$ cups	375 ml
$^1/_3$ cup + 1 tbs	90 ml	$1^3/_4$ cups	400 ml
$^1/_3$ cup + 2 tbs	100 ml	$1^3/_4$ cups + 2 tbs	450 ml
$^1/_2$ cup	120 ml	2 cups (1 pint)	475 ml
$^2/_3$ cup	150 ml	$2^1/_2$ cups	600 ml
$^3/_4$ cup	180 ml	3 cups	720 ml
$^3/_4$ cup + 2 tbs	200 ml	4 cups (1 quart)	945 ml

(1,000 ml is 1 liter)

weight conversions

U.S. / U.K.	Metric	U.S. / U.K.	Metric
1/2 oz	14 g	7 oz	200 g
1 oz	28 g	8 oz	227 g
1 1/2 oz	43 g	9 oz	255 g
2 oz	57 g	10 oz	284 g
2 1/2 oz	71 g	11 oz	312 g
3 oz	85 g	12 oz	340 g
3 1/2 oz	100 g	13 oz	368 g
4 oz	113 g	14 oz	400 g
5 oz	142 g	15 oz	425 g
6 oz	170 g	1 lb	454 g

oven temperature conversions

°F	Gas Mark	°C
250	1/2	120
275	1	140
300	2	150
325	3	165
350	4	180
375	5	190
400	6	200
425	7	220
450	8	230
475	9	240
500	10	260
550	Broil	290

index